Leadership
Performance
Coaching

Leadership Performance Coaching

ELLE ALLISON

LEAD+
LEARN
PRESS

ENGLEWOOD, COLORADO

The Leadership and Learning Center
317 Inverness Way South, Suite 150
Englewood, Colorado 80112
Phone 1.866.399.6019 | Fax 303.504.9417
www.LeadandLearn.com

Published by Lead + Learn Press, a division of Advanced Learning Centers, Inc.

Library of Congress Cataloging-in-Publication Data

Allison, Elle, 1960-
  Leadership performance coaching / Elle Allison.
      p. cm.
  Includes bibliographical references and index.
    ISBN 978-1-935588-09-2 (alk. paper)
  1. Mentors in education.   2. Educational leadership.   I. Title.
    LB1731.4.A446 2011
    371.2'011--dc22

                                                    2011012659

ISBN 978-1-935588-09-2

Printed in the United States of America

15 14 13 12 11   01 02 03 04 05 06 07

For Len, and for Olé and for 2010.

Contents

List of Exhibits

Preface

IN RECENT YEARS, more and more organizations have invested in coaching as a professional development approach for growing new leaders, supporting leaders in current positions, and helping leaders new to their positions get off to a great start.

The power of coaching as a professional development model became apparent to me in 1996 when I took a new position as director of school improvement at a regional education agency in Iowa. In this role, I was offered the opportunity to attend a series of leadership seminars at John Deere and Company, led by Paul Axtell. The seminars included coaching as a way to support implementation of the goals I wanted to achieve through my leadership role.

Although the seminars I attended at John Deere were intended to help me learn how to set up and lead projects for success, what I really loved was being coached. More than being coached, however, I loved accomplishing important projects that made a difference to me, the leaders I supported at that time, and my organization. My first coaching project, in fact, was to implement a learning academy for school principals. The main strategies I established led to powerful associations that last to this day with Michael Fullan and Gerry Smith (at that time, Gerry was principal of a model technology school in Toronto and a colleague of Dr. Fullan. Gerry is now Director of Professional Development at Apple). During the process of attending the seminars at John Deere, I discovered that being coached provided an essential support system. Coaching led me to achieve the goals I set for myself.

Leaders who want to accomplish great things in their work should not have to "go it alone." What if more leaders at all levels had a coach who would help them think through the most important decisions? What if more leaders at all levels had a regular opportunity to reflect on what they do to contribute to student achievement and empowerment, which, after all, is undoubtedly the most important outcome of educational systems worldwide (Reeves and Allison, 2010)?

Coaching is not a panacea. Coaching *is* a powerful method for developing leaders and organizations. This book is written for leaders who want to take advantage of coaching as a method for accomplishing work that matters to them and to their organizations. As a master coach, I am especially devoted to assuring that leaders are critical consumers of coaching and coaches. This book describes what leaders should expect from coaching. This book also encourages leaders to seek opportunities to coach their peers, colleagues, and the individuals they supervise.

Chapters One through Three introduce leaders to the power of coaching and to what it takes to create an organization that supports coaching. Chapters Four through Seven describe the coaching conversation and the tools leaders should expect coaches to use. Chapters Eight and Nine instruct leaders in methods for setting up projects that they could be coached on. Chapters Ten and Eleven illuminate important opportunities for coaching relationships, and Chapter Twelve provides guidance for leaders who feel called to coaching as a way to support and motivate others.

The primary message I hope leaders come away with, from reading this book, is that coaching, done well, will provide you with a performance edge. As leaders in education, you have the opportunity to positively impact the future through the lives of the students you touch. With coaching, leaders have more time and energy to lead well.

ELLE ALLISON
California, USA, 2011

About the Author

Elle Allison

ELLE ALLISON is cofounder and president of Renewal Coaching. Along with Douglas Reeves, she is author of the three-book series *Renewal Coaching: Sustainable Change for Individuals and Organizations* (2009, 2010). Elle's experience in education comes from positions as a teacher, assistant principal, principal, director of school improvement, and assistant superintendent. Elle is a graduate of the seventh National Staff Development (Learning Forward) Academy and is a member of the National Speakers Association. She earned her doctorate in Organizational Learning from the University of New Mexico, where she focused on issues related to coaching, consulting, wisdom, leadership, and personal and organizational change. Elle is cofounder of Renewal Coaching LLC, and is the founder of Wisdom Out, where her research, writings, and keynote addresses illuminate the nature of wisdom and develop a foundation for life strategies that assist individuals and organizations in achieving a greater good. Elle designs and leads seminars and keynotes for leaders who coach and coaches who lead. Elle can be reached at eallison@renewalcoaching.com.

Acknowledgments

MANY PEOPLE HAVE HELPED MAKE THIS BOOK POSSIBLE. I offer my appreciation and gratitude:

First, to my friend and colleague Douglas Reeves, founder of The Leadership and Learning Center and cofounder of Renewal Coaching LLC. Doug never wavers in his commitment to do what he can to make education systems strong, purposeful, and resilient so that all students succeed in learning and in their lives. Doug's wisdom can be seen in the greater good he has created on this planet; from building a school in Africa, to coaching a high school debate team, to getting on a plane every week to fly to clients who are inspired to lead change in their own communities, Doug makes a difference every day.

To Paul Axtell, who was my first coach, and who still coaches me on the projects that matter most to me today. Paul taught me how to be a coach and how to mentor other coaches. Paul inspired me to understand just how important listening is to every coaching relationship and, indeed, to any relationship that matters. Paul's influence placed me on the path to becoming a coach, and I am grateful to him for mentoring me and setting a standard of excellence that guides my work today.

To the 150 clients (you know who you are) whom I have coached over the last 20 years. My apologies to the first 25 and my gratitude to all of you. No one is a coach until they have coached. Thank you for allowing me to coach you and to learn from you.

To a number of my colleagues at The Leadership and Learning Center who allowed me to support them in the coaching they do: Robert Kuklis, Brett Gies, Debbie Lee, Lynn Howard, Laura Benson, Tracey Flach, Christy Kutz, David Nagel, Jay Trujillo, Roberta Pace, Mary Rubadeau, Angela Peery, Sherry Burcham, Lillian Hawkins, Lavonne Henry, Judy Ingram, Cynthia Leak-Mormon, and Jo Peters.

PART 1

The Power of Coaching

CHAPTER ONE

What Brings You to Coaching?

BIG IDEAS IN CHAPTER ONE

- ► Leaders who seek coaching seek a performance edge in the work they do and the outcomes they achieve.
- ► Leadership Performance Coaching is a strategy to support education leaders who want to accomplish outcomes for their organization.
- ► Educators who accomplish important projects have the opportunity to grow as leaders.
- ► Leaders who seek coaching are self-empowered and efficacious.
- ► Leaders who seek coaching want coaches who have excellent reputations and who are known for supporting accomplished leaders.

Educational leaders who seek coaching are leaders who are at the top of their game. They are leaders who recognize that coaching gives them a performance edge. Think, for example, of great athletes and professionals in the performing arts. These individuals consistently and diligently work with great coaches who have a knack for helping them stretch, improve, and continue to do better that which they already do well. Coaching is a superior strategy for supporting leaders in being great in the most important work they do. In education, these are leaders in classrooms, schools, districts, regions, states, and countries who are in the position every single day to elevate learning and the experience of learning for the learners who trust them to do so.

Remarkable Outcomes

Coaching is a strategy for accomplishing remarkable outcomes. Coaching provides a performance edge to those who want to go beyond the limits of their own minds. To coach is to partner in thought with others in service of the goals these individuals have set for themselves, with the additional responsibility of provoking them to want more, see new perspectives, and take powerful action that leads to change.

Coaching is an expensive development approach if all coachees want to do is check items off of a "to-do" list. Countless books about time management and avoiding procrastination offer advice and strategies galore for accomplishing the tasks that gather on various lists and irritate us until we make time to complete them. Anyone can read about these strategies and choose to apply them, if only time can be made to purchase and then read the books. Leadership Performance Coaching goes way beyond the "to-do" list.

Leadership Performance Coaching is an approach to supporting educators who have an important project to accomplish. A fundamental requirement of this method of coaching is the early identification of and commitment to a project that creates outcomes that benefit the organization. Throughout coaching, coaches ask coachees to engage in high-impact actions that are known to help successfully launch projects. Coachees identify these actions, which include learning, looking at evidence, paying attention to the needs of people, making critical decisions, and writing them up in a 100-Day Plan (Reeves and Allison, 2009 and 2010; Allison, 2010a). Additionally, Leadership Performance Coaches who work with educators ask coachees to reflect on their growth as leaders as they create outcomes that align with the mission of their organization. This approach infers an important value: Leaders do not learn how to lead by reading about it. Leaders learn to lead by doing important work and reflecting on it with the help of a skilled coach.

Are You Open to Being Coached?

As you will learn in subsequent chapters of this book, coaching is a different way of relating to other people. It is different from mentoring, from supervising, from consulting, and from teaching. Coaching is not a casual conversation, and it is not a close friendship, or what Doug Reeves calls "Norm the bar buddy" (Reeves, 2007)—the accommodating person who is more than happy to allow companions to gripe and vent (but never take action to change their situation) as long as the beer generously flows.

Leaders who seek and accept coaching are open to active engagement with another person who, if the person has internalized the qualities and skills of an excellent coach, will support them in thinking deeper and broader than they would if they did not have a coach. This means that leaders who seek coaching are forthcoming with their ideas and thoughts. Leaders must tell the person coaching them what they want to accomplish within their organization, in vivid detail, with nothing left unsaid. Therefore, leaders who accept coaching take risks. They have to be willing to reveal where they recognize the holes in their thinking and the plans that emerge from their thinking. In some work cultures, where leaders are expected not to make mistakes, this level of vulnerability is not the norm and therefore feels quite uncomfortable; a good coach provides a time and place where leaders who want to be coached can say everything that needs to be said without fear of ridicule, judgment, or violations of confidentiality.

Leaders who accept coaching also expect their coaches to hold them accountable for the actions they committed to at the end of each coaching conversation. Therefore, they treat their commitments seriously and follow through with initiating the steps needed to accomplish their goal.

In short, leaders who accept coaching understand that coaching requires them to initiate a meaningful project to focus the coaching, adapt plans to respond to the current context of their situation, and take action in order to develop and improve their organizations. Clearly, coaching is not just your average conversation.

Are you a good candidate for coaching? Before you engage a coach, it helps to take an honest look at yourself to determine if coaching is the right development model for you. The following inventory adapted from my work with Renewal Coaching (Allison, 2010a) allows you to honestly assess your openness and readiness for coaching. Consider the questions provided on the survey below and rate yourself according to the levels provided.

1. **I have ideas that could make a difference in my organization and I would love to take action to bring them to life.**

This is not me at all						This sounds exactly like me			
1	2	3	4	5	6	7	8	9	10

2. **I work in an organization that values leaders who take advantage of opportunities to grow.**

This is not me at all						This sounds exactly like me			
1	2	3	4	5	6	7	8	9	10

3. **Even though methods for accomplishing the work I do change, I have a clear and consistent vision of the mission of my organization.**

This is not me at all						This sounds exactly like me			
1	2	3	4	5	6	7	8	9	10

4. I often have great ideas about how to accomplish important work, but I also know that my ideas improve when I have the chance to think them through with another person.

This is not me at all							This sounds exactly like me		
1	2	3	4	5	6	7	8	9	10

5. I am eager to express myself to other people who have shown themselves to be trustworthy of hearing even my most incomplete ideas.

This is not me at all							This sounds exactly like me		
1	2	3	4	5	6	7	8	9	10

6. I make time to reflect on my work and the impact of my efforts on a daily basis and I treat this reflection time as I do any other important commitment on my calendar.

This is not me at all							This sounds exactly like me		
1	2	3	4	5	6	7	8	9	10

7. When I commit to action, I follow through.

This is not me at all							This sounds exactly like me		
1	2	3	4	5	6	7	8	9	10

8. I don't expect answers and advice from the people I ask to coach me.

This is not me at all							This sounds exactly like me		
1	2	3	4	5	6	7	8	9	10

9. I believe I have wisdom about what is needed in my work, and I enjoy discovering insights that I can apply and take responsibility for.

This is not me at all							This sounds exactly like me		
1	2	3	4	5	6	7	8	9	10

10. I am eager to focus my goals, experiment with strategies, take risks, and reflect on outcomes with another person who is committed to helping me do so.

This is not me at all							This sounds exactly like me		
1	2	3	4	5	6	7	8	9	10

If you answered all 10 of the questions in the survey with a rating of 9 or 10, you are an excellent candidate for coaching. If most of your ratings are 6 and below, you might find the coaching process quite challenging. Low ratings do not necessarily mean you should avoid working with a coach. In fact, with a strong coach, you could benefit tremendously from a development experience that is different from what is comfortable for you. It does mean that you will want to ask the coach to provide you with feedback about how you are doing as a coaching client and whether or not you are taking advantage of the tools and processes that make coaching powerful.

Finding a Coach

Great coaches use processes and tools that allow their coachees to accomplish important projects, grow in leadership, and engage in reflection that helps them maintain perspective. But how do leaders who want to work with a coach find one who will be great for them? According to some experts, leaders seek coaches who are recommended by trusted colleagues (O'Neill, 2000). A 2009 Pricewaterhouse Coopers study from the International Coach Federation indicates that coachees look for and select coaches who have an effective coaching method, have confidence as a coach, and who focus on action and accomplishment.

Some educational organizations maintain either a formal or informal cadre of peer coaches who will support others as part of their working day. Other educational organizations have contracts with groups of coaches who are external to their system in order to provide coaching services. Whether leaders work with an internal or an external coach, here are some guidelines to keep in mind when selecting a coach (Allison, 2010a):

1. Only work with coaches who have a reputation for confidentiality. Leaders who provide coaching for their peers and colleagues must have a good reputation as a leader and as a professional. This requirement does not guarantee great coaching, but it does provide some certainty that this coach respects people and is mindful of projecting a professional image.

2. Find out if the coaches you want to work with are obligated to provide information about their coachees to supervisors or other governing bodies. For example, if a board of education hires a coach for a superintendent, the coach may be under contract to provide information that comes from the coaching sessions with the superintendent back to the board. If they have a choice in the mater, coachees need to be certain they are comfortable with the terms of the contract.

3. Seek coaches who use a coaching process and can describe that process in detail.

4. Look for coaches who have advanced degrees or additional training in organizational and adult learning and theories of change. These credentials do not guarantee great coaching, but they certify a certain level of confidence that coaches have a deeper understanding of the workings of complex systems and the people in them.

5. Seek coaches who belong to a coaching learning community and who have a personal plan for developing themselves as a coach.

6. Look for coaches who require their coachees to accomplish projects and specific outcomes that are important to their role and to the organization. Without focus, coaching conversations can devolve into gripe sessions, or into sessions devoted

to dealing with the little fires that pop up in any given day but do not necessarily represent important work.

7. Work with coaches who have a reputation among successful leaders for being a great coach.

Let the Journey Begin

If coaching is a development model for supporting good leaders in doing more of, and a better job at, the work aligned with the mission of the organization, then imagine *your* educational organization filled with leaders who seek coaching and who provide coaching for their peers, colleagues, and the people they supervise. Imagine the outcomes coaching will produce for those leaders and their teams, staff members, and students.

The rest of the chapters in this book present the Leadership Performance Coaching model provided by coaches from The Leadership and Learning Center (see Appendix A for a list of frequently asked questions about coaching from The Leadership and Learning Center). Along the way, you will have the opportunity to reflect on how coaching can make a difference in your work and the joys and benefits of coaching the people you work with and lead.

Coaching opens a new way of being, leading, and accomplishing the most important work leaders do. Welcome to the journey.

Understanding Coaching

BIG IDEAS IN CHAPTER TWO

► Leadership Performance Coaching develops leaders in education and produces action toward achieving the goals of the organization.

► Leadership Performance Coaching is not venting, advising, judging, or evaluating. It is not always easy, and it is not passive.

► Leadership Performance Coaching is different from mentoring, consulting, training, and supervising.

Leadership Performance Coaching Defined

Coaching programs abound in every industry. A Google search reveals myriad coaching options for businesses, nonprofit organizations, education, and personal growth. There are coaching approaches specifically designed to improve relationships, to help with financial planning, to write that book you feel is inside of you, to become a better parent, or to realize your dearest goals in life. Often, these coaching options draw on specific theories and philosophies. For example, there are coaching programs that draw on emotional intelligence, neuropsychology, cognitive behavioral theory, and organizational development, to name just a few. When people learn that coaching can give them and their organization a performance edge, they are likely to search for a coach with a perspective that best matches their context and specific needs (Reeves and Allison, 2009).

Leadership Performance Coaching is a coaching approach designed to support leaders in education. The definition of Leadership Performance Coaching (LPC) reveals the purpose of this particular coaching approach: "LPC is a series of conversations that helps leaders develop the skills they need to communicate their vision, motivate and mobilize people, monitor indicators, and produce results through others. LPC is action-oriented, to achieve goals that matter" (Allison, 2010b, p.13).

The relevance of the definition becomes clear when we examine each segment of it. When we analyze the definition, we clearly see that coaching is a strategy for developing leaders as they accomplish important projects that advance the goals of the organization. Exhibit 2.1 separates each segment and explains the related ideas.

What Leadership Performance Coaching Is Not

Just as we find value in examining the definition of LPC, it is equally beneficial to explore what LPC is not. The following four explanations about what LPC is not can help us discern the qualities of LPC.

1. **LPC is not a series of venting sessions.** At the start of a coaching conversation, coaches ask coachees to tell them how they are doing and how their project is going. Specifically, coaches ask coachees to tell the story about how they were able to carry out the actions they identified at the end of the previous coaching conversation. When things have gone well, the conversation begins with celebration. When the stories coachees have to tell are full of angst and frustration, however, the temptation to vent is great. Focused and brief venting at the start of a coaching conversation does have a purpose. Venting allows coachees to let off emotional steam and

Leadership Performance Coaching Defined

Definition Segment	Meaning and Implications
LPC is a series of conversations...	LPC most often occurs between two people who have an ongoing relationship. They engage with each other, using a specific conversation format that allows the coachee (the person being coached) to wrestle with important ideas and arrive at a place of action.
...that helps leaders develop the skills they need to communicate their vision, motivate and mobilize people, monitor indicators, and produce results through others.	As coachees engage in coaching, they simultaneously develop leadership abilities. During the course of accomplishing important projects within their organization and through their role, coachees become aware of their leadership strengths and challenges and mindfully deepen the first and confront the second.
LPC is action-oriented, to achieve goals that matter.	The coaching process leads to action. LPC is a strategy for accomplishing important work that advances the organization. The coaching projects are specific and coachees are responsible for accomplishing them. The projects identified by coachees must also serve the needs of the organization. These projects go way beyond the coachee's "to-do list." They are projects that matter long term and for significant stakeholders. In education, all coaching projects inevitably need to make a difference for students, either by directly impacting students (such as implementing differentiated instruction, for example) or by directly impacting the adults and structures in the system, which allows better service to students (such as implementing Data Teams, for example).

helps to clear the way for new thoughts. Venting also signals the emotional state of coachees to their coaches, and this provides coaches with information that may be useful during the coaching conversation. However, venting is unproductive, and signifies a lack of resilience when it continues past the first few minutes of the conversation (Allison, 2010a). Coaching should always lead to action and a sense of efficacy. Prolonged venting will prevent the coaching conversation from achieving this purpose.

2. LPC is not advice-giving. Coaches who cannot overcome the need to dispense advice and offer opinions undermine the powerful impact of great coaching. Coachees may politely listen to advice, but they rarely follow it. Savvy coachees eventually tire of giving over their coaching session to coaches who use the precious time available to show just how smart and experienced they are. Great coaches understand that they cannot entirely apprehend the complexity of the living system the coachee interacts with each day (Allison, 2010a). No matter how experienced the coach is, even if the coach does exactly the same work as the coachee, the coachee's context will be different from what the coach knows from personal experience, and the solutions that work for the coach will not necessarily work for the coachee. LPC is a strategy for developing leaders, not for creating dependencies in others (Reeves and Allison, 2009).

3. LPC is not judgment and evaluation. Although Leadership Performance Coaching can be used as a follow-up strategy for supporting leaders in their professional growth, it is not itself an evaluation system. At the same time, evaluations and performance reviews, especially when they contain feedback from supervisors or boards about strengths and challenges in leadership, provide data that coaches and coachees can look at together and use to focus the goals of the coaching project. This being said, the coaching process itself is devoid of judgment. Keeping with the premise that great coaches do not offer advice, coaches also do not issue judgments of right or wrong, good or bad, or smart or foolish when coachees share their ideas. Instead, coaches ask open-ended and sometimes provocative questions that allow their coachees to fully explore their ideas and inclinations and evaluate them for their impact on the system.

4. LPC is not one-sided or passive. Over the course of the coaching relationship, both coaches and coachees work hard. Coaches are expected to be great at coaching and coachees are expected to identify an important project through which they can create benefits for their organization and deepen their leadership. Great coaches use a process for moving coachees toward action and impact. They employ deliberate and advanced skills in listening, summarizing, clarifying, questioning, and calling for action. Coaches create trusting conditions where coachees can say anything, even what scares them or where they think they have gone wrong. Coachees on the other hand, must be willing to take action and talk about the challenges and victories that mark the journey to change.

Different Ways of Supporting Others: Coaching, Mentoring, Consulting, and Training

Coaching is different from other ways of supporting people. Knowing the differences eliminates all sorts of misunderstanding and clarifies the outcomes of the coaching relationship (Allison, 2010a). Without this understanding, coaches lack a firm foundation from which to carry out the coaching, and coachees may feel like they are not getting what they think they should out of the relationship. For example, when coachees confuse coaching with mentoring, they expect the coach to speak from their own experience and give advice. When coachees confuse coaching with consulting, they expect the coach to provide them with their assessment of the situation and to offer recommendations. When coachees confuse coaching with training, they expect their coach to tell them or show them how to perform certain tasks or provide information and knowledge. When coachees confuse coaching with supervising, they expect their coach to rate their performance and to make judgments about whether or not they are meeting expectations and performing to a set of standards (Allison, 2010a; Landsberg, 2003; O'Neill, 2000; Reeves and Allison, 2009).

Savvy coachees who expect to be coached toward accomplishing their most important goals will find coaches who lack clarity on the differences between these approaches outrageously inadequate (Allison, 2010a). Coaches who do not understand what it means to be a coach will mindlessly advise, offer opinions, allow unproductive griping and venting, and use the coaching time to share their own stories and experiences.

This is not to say that mentoring, consulting, training, and supervising do not have a role in developing others. However, understanding the differences between these approaches and coaching is critical not only to the process of development that each approach catalyzes, but to achieve the specialized outcomes of each approach.

Let's take a closer look at each strategy, determine what they have in common, and further illuminate what makes coaching unique.

First, all of these approaches have some important strategies in common. Whether you are coaching, supervising, mentoring, consulting, or training, all of these approaches provide development opportunities for individuals, organizations, or both, and all of these approaches require high levels of skill in listening, clarifying, summarizing, paraphrasing, and questioning.

The differences between these development approaches are best seen through analysis of the role, purpose, desired outcome, client, and the duration of the relationship. Exhibit 2.2 provides a visual comparison of the characteristics of coaching, mentoring, consulting, training, and supervising.

LPC and Blending of Other Approaches

Some education organizations decide to offer a comprehensive support system to individuals who are new to their roles, in which the coach or mentor skillfully recognizes when the coachee or mentee needs a particular approach and then operates from that paradigm. In fact, Leadership Performance Coaching applies a coaching conversation process (described in detail in Chapter Four) that provides room for coaches to engage in aspects of consulting, teaching, and mentoring, depending on the need of the coachee. However, when coaches activate these other roles within a coaching relationship, they need to do so transparently. For example, in the last half to last quarter of a coaching conversation, after coachees have wrestled with the challenging issues of their situation, coaches will ask, "What are you thinking now?" If the coachee responds to this question with frustration and confusion, the coach may choose to switch to a consultant role, for example, by saying something like, "May I share with you how other leaders in your position have responded effectively to this issue?"

In the same way, a coach may don an instructional hat while using a coaching approach, by offering tools and resources that the coachee can use. Again, however, coaches should switch to this role only toward the end of the coaching conversation and only after coachees have made commitments to actions they wish to take to move their projects forward (Allison, 2010a). For example, let's say a high school principal wants to have a conversation with the Data Team leader in the math department. The coach might actually have a useful protocol or tool for looking at the requirements for looking at data. It would be ludicrous to deprive the coachee of this valuable tool. So, the coach asks if the coachee wants to have a copy of it. If the coachee says yes, then the coach has the green light to go ahead and, within this coaching relationship, provide didactic instructions about how to use the data collection tool, as the coach has used it in other similar situations.

Undisciplined coaches, who default to the approach they find most comfortable (mentoring, advising, training, supervising), may not be coaching as much as they think they are. As previously mentioned (and will be fully explored in Chapter Four), coaches use a conversation flow that maps out the places in the coaching engagement

EXHIBIT 2.2   Characteristics of Coaching, Mentoring, Consulting, Training, and Supervising

	Coaching	Mentoring	Consulting	Training	Supervising
Role	Thought partner	Guide and critical friend. A senior expert.	Advisor	Teacher	Evaluator
Purpose	Provide a process that offers a performance edge to leaders who want to go beyond the limitations of their own thought processes.	Offer advice, and help the mentee avoid missteps and pitfalls inherent in their role, the culture and the expectations of the organization and profession.	Examine evidence, diagnose the situation, provide feedback, and recommend solutions.	Present learning experiences that provide participants with the opportunity to learn and deepen knowledge and skills, and apply them in their work.	Assure accomplishment of important expectations and hold accountable for results. Provide judgment and feedback about how well employees are doing according to a set of standards or specific expectations.
"Client"	An individual at any level within the system who wants to accomplish important goals and deepen his or her efficacy and capacity for doing great work.	An individual who is a novice to his or her role, job, or to the organization.	A "contracting client." Someone who requests another person or group to provide solutions.	A person who wants to learn specific skills or gain knowledge to use in his or her work.	An employee who reports to the supervisor.

EXHIBIT 2.2 Characteristics of Coaching, Mentoring, Consulting, Training, and Supervising *continued*

	Coaching	Mentoring	Consulting	Training	Supervising
Desired Outcome	The individual accomplishes important projects that advance the organization and create a context for deepening leadership abilities.	The mentee is inducted into their role to the extent that they are aware of the expectations, have resolution to questions, understand the expectations of the culture and of written policies and procedures, and can navigate the system with success in order to do their best work.	The contracting client chooses to accept or reject the recommendations of the consultant, in whole or part, for the good of the organization.	The participant applies best practices and knowledge in the work he or she does.	The employee improves and ultimately excels in the expectations defined for his or her position.
Duration	Coaching can continue throughout a person's career and life, either with the same coach or with different coaches as long as the coachee has important work to accomplish and he or she believes that coaching would provide a performance edge.	Mentoring usually ends within two years, or when both parties agree the mentee is knowledgeable about the culture, organization, and the expectations of his or her role.	The consulting period is clearly defined in advance and documented in the consulting contract. The consultant does not usually have further obligation to the client once the contract is completed.	Can be provided at different levels of need and over brief or extended periods. Clients with a philosophy of life-long learning engage in training experiences and learning opportunities for their entire careers.	Continues to some extent for the duration of an employee's tenure.

where blending other approaches is indicated. This process provides a safeguard that at the very least causes coaches to recognize where they are tempted to consult, collaborate, or teach, simply because these approaches are easier or have become habit.

In summary, coaching is a development strategy for supporting leaders who want to accomplish remarkable outcomes in order to advance the mission and goals of their organization. Coaching is different from mentoring, consulting, training, and supervising, although all of these approaches utilize the same communication skills, to varying degrees. Leadership Performance Coaches are disciplined and mindful about how they interact with coachees, and they transparently and appropriately employ the benefits from approaches other than coaching, in service of supporting their coachees.

The Coaching Organization

BIG IDEAS IN CHAPTER THREE

► Leaders expect coaching to serve the goals of the organization.

► Organizations need to align their practices and cultures to structures and attitudes that support coaching.

► Coaching is a strategy for supporting implementation of organizational initiatives and strategies to meet system goals.

► Coaching creates a learning organization.

The Power of Coaching

My favorite question to ask leaders and decision makers is this: What could happen if more leaders supported other leaders in accomplishing the most important goals of the organization? In educational organizations the answers paint a promising picture and include the following outcomes:

- "We would retain our best principals."
- "Teacher effectiveness would increase."
- "We would develop better leaders from within our teacher ranks."

• "Student achievement would improve."

More research is needed about the impact of coaching on these key indicators in education. In an exit survey of educational leaders who worked with coaches from The Leadership and Learning Center, many said they completed the project they asked to be coached on sooner than they would have without a coach, and felt more confidence in their ability to do their work. They also said that they believed their organization benefited directly from the projects they were coached on (Allison, 2009).

In light of the known and the predicted outcomes of coaching, leaders need to take some time to reflect on their organization's capacity to successfully operate a leadership coaching program.

Is Your Organization Ready for Coaching?

Many leaders say they want a coaching program in their organizations. But not all organizations have a culture fully aligned with the purpose of coaching. Coaches and coachees who find themselves operating in organizations that are not fully prepared to support the coaching process and what comes out of coaching for their employees, should be aware of barriers they may need to work around or remove.

The late Peter Drucker, who is accepted as the father of management, counsels leaders with the adage that "culture eats strategy for breakfast." What this means, of course, is that an organization can implement the best strategies known but they will fail if the culture is not simultaneously built to support the strategy implementation. Organizations that invest in coaching need to create a culture that supports coaching. These organizations need to audit their culture for the attitudes, patterns of interaction, policies, and practices that support coaching. They need to shore up the organization with cultural structures that support coaching and eliminate or revise existing structures that hinder a healthy culture for coaching.

Many educational organizations have histories of failed or short-lived initiatives. Leadership Performance Coaching is an initiative like any other. It must be understood, supported both in theory and in application, and it must be prioritized to receive resources. The truth is, not all organizations have a culture fully aligned with the purposes of coaching, Decision makers who want to add coaching as a development strategy for leaders in their organization need to be aware of the practices and cultural norms that support coaching and seek to remove the barriers that will diminish the benefits of coaching. If they do not, coaching, like other initiatives, will fail to thrive.

The following checklist is adapted from my work in Renewal Coaching and reflects the organizational practices and cultural norms that allow coaching to work (Allison, 2010a). Where are your organization's strengths and challenges? Read the sentences in Exhibit 3.1 and check each of them off as either a strength or a challenge. When you complete the checklist on your own, check your assumptions with at least two other people with whom you work.

Because coaching is a strategy for sustaining the best initiatives, *and* is a powerful innovation in its own right (Reeves and Allison, 2009), organizations that make coaching work reap exponential benefits. If your organization is primed to support coaching, each and every one of your other initiatives will benefit. Let's take a closer look at the ways an organization benefits from coaching.

Coaching Promotes Learning and Teaching between Adults

Within the coaching relationship, coaches and coachees give and receive, learn and teach. This makes coaching highly reciprocal in nature, with a focus on promoting the best elements of a learning organization (Reeves and Allison, 2009 and 2010). Educational organizations that utilize peer leadership coaching promote meaningful exchanges of knowledge about what matters most within the organization and how to best accomplish what matters most. Not only do coaches learn more about the work of the people they coach,

Determing Your Organization's Strengths and Challenges

Strength   **Challenge**

_____   _____   1. People in our organization trust each other.

_____   _____   2. People in our organization know they can explore new ideas and take risks in alignment with our mission.

_____   _____   3. Our organization provides time and space for job-embedded professional development.

_____   _____   4. People in our organization are focused on achieving the goals of the organization.

_____   _____   5. We believe that leaders at all levels grow by taking action and reflecting on the impact their actions have on student achievement.

_____   _____   6. Our organization prioritizes time for professionals to think and experiment together.

_____   _____   7. We believe that reflection is essential to awareness and leads to innovation and renewal of people and programs.

_____   _____   8. People in our organization know they can bring anything up for discussion.

_____   _____   9. People in our organization completely understand the organization's mission and goals and want to take initiative to contribute.

_____   _____   10. People in our organization respect the ideas of others.

and coachees come to better understand and become effective in their work, but coachees begin to pick up the communication skills they experience with their coach and use them in their interactions with others. At the same time, with each and every opportunity coaches have to coach, they deepen and expand their capacity for coaching.

Organizational Development

Conventional ideas of coaching tend to be limited to the idea that it is a productive professional relationship between a coach and a coachee that allows the coachee to become a better leader and accomplish important projects. I encourage leaders to go beyond the limits of this assumption and consider how coaching can lead to whole organizational change and development.

"Mike" was Assistant Superintendent of Curriculum and Instruction in a medium-sized urban school district. Three years ago, Mike asked to be coached on a project that was near and dear to his heart. He wanted to form an alliance with the state university to make his district a welcoming and rigorous destination for student teachers. He envisioned his district being known for providing extraordinary support for student teachers, while they learned under the guidance of the best teachers in the district. Mike's vision included the idea that these student teachers would choose to seek teaching positions within the district once they graduated from the university.

As Mike took action within his coaching project, he discovered an unexpected opportunity to restructure the long-standing practice in the district of assigning the best teachers to the classes with the highest-performing students. The opportunity arose out of conversations with the university professors, who had a pilot program to prepare novice teachers who specifically wanted to make a difference in closing achievement gaps between students in urban settings. The professors needed strong student teaching placements for these individuals. Mike was keen to step up and meet this need, even though his best teachers, and those who would be powerful mentors to the student teachers, were not necessarily assigned to the most challenging classrooms in the district. In fact, he knew that the "toughest" classes were staffed with the most novice teachers in the district.

Bolstered by his coaching sessions, Mike enlisted the support of two teachers who responded with passion and excitement to his proposal that they take on these student teachers and work with them within the most challenging classes in the district. Some of the perks Mike wrangled for these teachers in addition to the usual stipend included two extra planning periods per week and specialized professional development.

Through his coaching project, Mike found himself leading an initiative that challenged and partially unhinged one of the most destructive, yet unquestioned, practices of the district. Although the practice of assigning novice teachers to the most challenging classes still occurs in his district on occasion, more people there are talking about how ridiculous a practice it really is. Mike is now working at multiple levels within the system, including with the teacher's union, to eliminate the practice altogether.

From Mike's story, we see that coaching is more than an individual leadership development strategy. A single coaching project can transform the entire organization.

Coaching Creates Learning Organizations

Coaching always leads to action through reflection. Each coaching session ends with the question, "What will you do next?" And, each *new* coaching conversation begins with a question from the coach that asks, in one way or another, "How did those actions turn out?" These two simple questions catalyze action leadership and reflection (Allison, 2010a) and are hallmarks of learning organizations. Moreover, schools and districts that embrace coaching make visible two important values that other organizations merely give lip service to—even if they agree to them in principle. These are the values of action and reflection (Fullan, 2009).

Organizations that support a coaching culture make action and reflection visible (Senge, et al., 1994). These organizations embrace coaching as a development strategy, offer coaching to leaders, schedule time for coaching, and document the benefits and outcomes, relating them to specific organizational goals. Time for reflection is uncommon in most workplaces, and especially so in education, where the complex demands of the system compete for the energy that is needed to focus on teaching and learning in the classroom. Coaching, by its very nature, provides the time and space needed for the sort of reflective conversations that always lead to insight and action about the important work at hand. In fact, the coaching conversation itself is artfully designed to lead to clarity of leadership action (see Chapter Four: The Coaching Conversation). Coaching also provides time and space for leaders to hear their own thoughts, make sense out of confusion, and determine the next action steps.

The support that coaching demands from organizations in order to be successful also defines the benefits returned to organizations from coaching. Exhibit 3.2 captures ideas about what coaching demands from organizations and what it returns to the organization to further define and develop it as a learning organization.

Organizations that employ effective coaching programs *are* learning organizations. Leaders in organizations that embrace coaching and create cultures to support the best outcomes of coaching possess an elegant and impactful strategy for supporting current leaders, developing new leaders, and embedding learning into the workday.

Learning organizations resonate strongly with the structure of coaching conversations that help leaders move to action. In the next chapter, we look at the steps in the coaching conversation process and learn why they are effective.

Coaching Requirements and Benefits

What Coaching Requires of Organizations	How Organizations Develop as a Result of Coaching
Coaching is a development process that requires resources such as people, time, and energy.	Leaders who receive coaching change and grow in their leadership ability.
Coaching asks leaders to focus on a single project.	Leaders launch and implement critical projects that align with the mission of the organization and move it forward toward excellence.
Coaching demands time from coaches and coachees to engage in regular coaching conversations.	Leaders uncover their own wisdom about how to face challenges, solve dilemmas, and accomplish worthy outcomes.
Coaching holds coachees accountable for taking action.	Leaders reflect on the impact of their actions and modify and refine their approaches in order to create the best outcomes and the greatest gains.
Coaching requires coachees to make changes and improvements to the processes they use to accomplish important work and achieve outcomes.	Leaders become smarter about how to do important work and achieve outcomes that align with the mission of the organization.

PART 2

The Tools and Processes of the Coaching Conversation

The Coaching Conversation

BIG IDEAS IN CHAPTER FOUR

► The coaching conversation process is the framework used in every coaching episode. It is designed to lead coachees to knowledge of specific actions to move their project forward.

► Coachees count on coaches to have a process and method that guarantees productive coaching.

► Every coaching conversation begins with account-ability and ends with a commitment to action.

The Importance of Process

Although Leadership Performance Coaching is much more than a conversation between a coach and a coachee, the conversation makes the coaching process both visible and tangible. Each coaching episode is a professional interaction between two people, both of whom care deeply, although for different reasons, about the topic at hand. These conversations are scheduled well in advance and treated with the same regard given to other critical meetings or professional development opportunities. Both parties understand that quality coaching has a profound impact on producing outcomes that contribute to the mission of the coachee's school, district, or organization (Joyce and Showers, 1995); therefore, both parties consider the conversation a priority.

The coaching conversation has an elegant design. It leads coachees from their current reality, where the next steps of their project are unclear or undefined, to a new reality in which they know the best actions to take next, and feel confident in taking them. This is not to suggest that coachees are always confused about what to do; sometimes they simply have not had one reflective moment during their demanding day to fully develop their ideas around the project. Whether or not coachees feel stress about knowing what actions will best move their project forward, having the opportunity to hear and understand their own thoughts, in the company of a skilled and compassionate coach, is an oasis in a day devoid of the opportunity to reflect.

According to the 2009 International Coach Federation Global Coaching Client Study by Pricewaterhouse Coopers, the effectiveness of the coaching process is one of the top attributes that coachees look for in their coaches. Coachees depend on coaches to bring a coaching methodology to the partnership that will allow them to accomplish their goals. If the coaching process is to be effective for coachees, coaches must use the conversation process with trust and confidence.

How the Coaching Conversation Process Works

Formal coaching agreements result in a contract between the coach and the coachee for a set number of coaching sessions over a defined time period. In addition, Leadership Performance Coaching (LPC) requires coachees to identify a project they wish to be coached on (see Chapter Nine for details about setting up the coaching project). Once these two requirements (the coaching agreement, and the coaching project) have been met, the scheduled coaching conversations begin and the coach activates the coaching conversation process.

The coaching conversation process is not a script. Nor, in spite of its presentation as a flowchart starting at the top of the page and ending at the bottom, is it meant to impose a rigid and linear exchange. Instead, the flow defines the space and time parsed over about 60 minutes, during which the coach matches the coachee's developing thought process with specific communication approaches known for the powerful way they enhance and provoke the sort of thinking that leads to empowerment. On paper, the process is presented in a linear format (Exhibit 4.1). This allows us to discuss and understand each part of the coaching conversation in relationship to the whole. In reality, the coaching conversation is dynamic and the coaching conversation process adapts and readapts as coach and coachee traverse the ground between not knowing what to do and knowing what to do.

The order of communication tools presented in the coaching conversation process flow is not accidental. Coaches who, out of their own anxiety or need for solutions, rush the early steps to get to the brainstorming and commitment-to-action steps, diminish the power of coaching and nearly guarantee frustration for the coachees, who feel they are being manipulated.

Step 1: Greetings and Accountability

Step 1, Greetings and Accountability, provides space for coaches and coachees to greet each other and welcome each other to the conversation. This reignites the rapport between them, which grows and deepens with each new interaction. Step 1 also includes coaches asking coachees to refer back to the actions they committed to at the end of the previous coaching conversation. This request and focus early in the coaching conversation signals the importance that both parties place on the power of coaching. With this question, right from the start, coaches convey an assumption of action and accountability on the part of coachees. More importantly, they convey their belief in the coachee's efficacy and empowerment. It is as if coaches are saying, "Of course I know you are a leader who follows through on commitments and takes action." If coaches discover coachees who rarely if ever follow through on commitments, they will point it out and may even ask to focus a coaching session on this particular barrier. But that situation aside, step 1 is crucial for establishing rapport and for the coachee to catch the coach up on all that has transpired related to the project that is the focus and purpose of the coaching.

When, in step 1, coachees speak about how the actions they took affected the project, coaches just listen and resist interrupting the flow of the story with questions and comments. Instead, coaches take notes and notice ways in which the project seems to be moving forward, where the snags appear, and what their coachees think and feel about the whole thing. During this phase, and certainly throughout the coaching relationship, coaches refrain from asking questions out of personal curiosity or "need to know." As coachees come to the end of the story, coaches summarize what seems to be the status of the project as related by their coachees. This signals movement into step 2, which invites the coachees to declare the focus of *this particular* coaching conversation.

Step 2: Focus the Conversation

In step 1, we see coachees catching coaches up on what has transpired over the past week or two between coaching sessions. Step 2, on the other hand, thrusts the coach and coachee back into the present moment. Step 2 acknowledges the events that took place in the life of coachees between coaching sessions, but more to the point, it focuses today's conversation in light of what took place. In step 2, coaches ask coachees to identify the goal of the current conversation. Presumably, if the coaching conversation is successful, it will meet the goal of the session and lead coachees once again to knowing what to do next to move their project forward and achieve the desired outcomes.

LPC employs the use of a 100-day project to inspire coachees to premeditate high-impact actions known to be crucial to the successful initiative launch (Reeves and Allison, 2009 and 2010). These actions are the sort that, if ignored, would be sure to undermine the project. They include, for example, collecting and analyzing data, using evidence to make decisions, communicating the vision, enlisting key stakeholders, conducting research, and experimenting, to name a few. Unfortunately, even veteran leaders occasionally undervalue the importance of predetermining and timing high-impact actions. Without a 100-day plan, they are left only with hindsight, which gives them a clear view of where they took a wrong turn or neglected to take an obvious step (Allison, 2010a).

The 100-day plan is a tool for maintaining a crisp focus on the coachee's project. In step 2, coaches refer to the 100-day plan, and together coaches and coachees review the intended progression of actions, comparing them to the reality of the project as it has unfolded in real time. In this way, the 100-day plan is flexible, yet it keeps reminding coachees about the high-impact actions they might overlook in the heat of responding to the inevitable challenges that come up along the way.

Step 2 gives coachees the choice to either focus on the premeditated high-impact actions or to address what has come up, but is still related to the forward movement of the coaching project. For example, on occasion, coachees find themselves facing leadership adversities and forces of resistance or politics that sap their energy for the project if they don't have the opportunity to address them. In these circumstances, the coaching session focuses on supporting coachees in facing and resolving each adversity so that they can refocus and reenergize for their project (Allison, 2010a).

Step 3: Listen

After coachees express the desired goal of the current coaching conversation, coaches invite them to talk about it. The coach just listens. In step 3, listening is the primary tool used by the coach. In fact, it is not overstating its importance to say that listening is *the* most important tool of every great coach.

Paul Axtell, who was my first coach and who also trained me in coaching, describes the listening that occurs in step 3 of the coaching conversation as listening with nothing added, nothing altered, nothing resisted, and nothing judged. Great coaches embrace these ideas and even adopt them as guiding values when it comes to listening. To listen with nothing added, nothing altered, nothing resisted, and nothing judged is to listen from a rock-solid foundation that disallows terrible communication habits such as interrupting, taking over the story, and inserting comments about what you think and feel. None of these habits are productive in a coaching relationship, and they are not very helpful in other relationships either (Nichols, 1995).

During step 3, coaches listen. This means that during the listening phase of the coaching conversation, the coach really and truly keeps quiet. Until the coachee has completely said all that needs to be said, the coach refrains from asking questions or making comments. The idea that they have to listen for a little while, without interrupting, making comments, or asking questions, makes new coaches-in-training squirm. They simply are not used to listening in this unique way, so it feels awkward and even impolite. But when they let go and finally trust me enough as their facilitator (or perhaps just to humor me), they discover the magical role that listening plays in coaching. Many people go for days and days without anyone in their lives really listening to them. This reality deprives them of hearing and "seeing" their own thoughts. When coaches listen to coachees in the unique way called for in step 3 of the coaching conversation, coachees actually begin to see new realities, and some even begin to untie sticky issues and see solutions. All of this, and the coach has not uttered a word.

Coaches who deprive themselves of listening to their coachees in step 3 of the coaching conversation also do themselves a grave disservice. Coaches who do not listen are left only with their own thoughts, opinions, and experiences about their coachees' issues. When it comes time for these coaches who have not listened well to speak and ask important questions (steps 4 and 5), they have nothing relevant to draw on. Because they have not listened, these coaches will only be able to speak from their point of view and will not be able to speak in service of the coachees. If coaches allow this to happen, they have popped out of the coaching role and can only deliver a monologue of their own ideas. This is not what coachees expect or deserve from coaching. If they wanted information and opinions, they would read a book or attend a lecture.

Step 4: Deepen Understanding

In step 3, coaches listen, which puts them in the perfect position to effectively engage in the coaching skills required in step 4.

Step 4 requires coaches to ask clarifying and detail questions about what the coachees have brought up so far, and to offer summaries and paraphrases of what seem to be the most important aspects and essence of the story the coachees told in step 3. In step 4, coaches seek to deeply understand their coachees' situations. They demonstrate this understanding by asking for details and clarification about what seem to be the most important aspects of the story told to them by their coachees. The effect this has on the coachees is palpable. To be understood by another human being who cares about our life and work is to be treated as if we matter. When someone understands our challenges, opportunities, hopes, desires, and dilemmas, we feel less alone and more able to see our way through what previously seemed unique or even peculiar to us. Suddenly, someone else "gets us," and because they are not judging or resisting the story, they legitimize the way we see it at this point in time. With this starting point, the coaching conversation can move on to step 5, which is the introduction of mediating questions that provoke, excite, and engage the coachee at a completely different level.

Step 5: Interact Through Questions

Step 5 begins when coaches and coachees feel that the work of step 4 is complete—in other words, when coaches feel that they deeply understand the situation, and coachees feel deeply understood. Great coaches end step 4 with a summary statement that coachees resonate with. Coaches know this because their coachees usually say something like, "You've captured the main issues beautifully." Coaches enter step 5 by saying something to the effect of, "Now that we have good understanding of what's going on for you, let me ask you some open-ended questions that will allow you to further illuminate your thinking." Of course, you don't have to use these exact words. The point is, because the type of questions you ask in step 5 of the coaching conversation are so different from the questions you ask in step 4 (which are more "close-ended," asking for specific details or clarification about what has been said so far), it helps to announce the transition from step 4 to step 5. In step 5, coachees think bigger, broader, and beyond what they currently understand and feel.

Step 5 gets to the heart of understanding coaching as mediation of thought (Costa and Garmston, 1994). Through the skillful application of open-ended mediating questions that engage various thinking and emotional processes, coaches help coachees to expand and shift their perspective. Coachees begin to experience breakthrough insights—what Garmston and Costa call "cognitive shifts." They may suddenly understand what is missing and what is important, and they come to understand events within a systemic context.

While reflecting on and responding to the mediating questions put on the table by their coaches, coachees often have stunning new insights and ideas. This is also the time in the coaching conversation when coachees can run models and scenarios about actions they wish to take or need to take to move their project forward. In the safety of the coaching relationship, they can take risks and explore the best and worst of what could happen in the real workplace.

Step 5 of the coaching conversation begins to wind down when coachees have expressed new insights and reflected on how they shift the current reality described in step 3. Sometimes this means they have completely revised the original story because during the course of responding to the coaches' questions, they have uncovered a more relevant, nuanced reality.

As coachees settle into these new understandings, they pause a bit longer and sometimes express amazement at what they now understand. They might say something like, "Hmm. It is quite interesting how I now see my situation!" Statements like this clue coaches to move the coaching conversation on to steps 6 and 7, which sometimes happen in a fast and furious manner, especially when coachees have experienced exciting and engaging breakthrough thoughts.

Step 6: Reflect and Brainstorm

Step 6 begins with the acknowledgement that, as a result of the conversation so far, the coachee now has a new perspective and/or has moved forward toward the goal. It invites coachees to identify where they see inroads and ways in which they can leverage action to move their project forward. Step 6 also invites brainstorming and possibility by asking coachees to think aloud about what they see that they could do. During this step, coaches go back to using the great coaching skills they have employed thus far, including listening, asking for details or clarification as needed, and summarizing and paraphrasing what seem to be the important ideas.

Step 7: Commit to Action

As the coaching conversation proceeds toward conclusion, coaches move to step 7 in which coaches ask coachees to commit to action. By this point in the coaching conversation, and if coaches have skillfully and mindfully activated the tools along the way, coachees usually have clarity about the next actions to take that will move their project forward. Coaches introduce this step by saying something along the lines of, "Well, we are reaching the end of our time together, and you've identified several actions you could take now. What actions will you commit to taking between now and our next conversation?" Coaches support coachees in committing to somewhere between one and three actions. These actions often involve other people, but they are actions coachees can take to influence the system they work within.

At the end of the coaching conversation, coaches can offer to send coachees journal articles or tools, if they have them, to support the actions their coachees commit to. Coaches do not add to the list of actions that the coachees have chosen to take. If the coach gives "homework," it is either something to read or reflect on directly related to the actions the coachee wishes to take, or to leadership challenges that came up during the course of the conversation. Coaches also use the final moment of the conversation to summarize the one to three actions committed to by the coachees and to ask for feedback about the coaching session itself. They might ask, "How did this session work for you? Is there anything I could do more of or less of for you as your coach?" (Axtell, 2009). In addition, coaches will mention the date and time of the next coaching conversation and make sure that the coachees have the same date and time written on their calendar.

The role of the coach during the final moments of the conversation is to resonate positive energy that conveys belief in the abilities and gifts of the coachee (Reeves and Allison, 2009 and 2010; Allison, 2010a). Coaches must take care not to undermine the hard work that has led to the moment of commitment by disagreeing with or second-guessing the wisdom of their coachees' decisions. Why should they? When coaches mindfully engage in the art and science of coaching, they can trust that their coachees will move forward in the important work they do with insight and confidence. Coaches cannot prevent their coachees from experiencing pain during those times when things do not go as the coachees planned or hoped. But they can choose to provide great coaching that supports their coachees in finding value in each success and each challenge.

EXHIBIT 4.1

The Coaching Conversation Process

Step 1: Greetings and Accountability

"How did the actions you committed to at the end of the last conversation work out?"

⬇

Step 2: Focus the Conversation

"What actions do you have listed next on your 100-day plan? Do you want to be coached on this or is there something different related to your project that you would like to be coached on?"

⬇

Step 3: Listen

"Tell me about that situation." (Coach just listens.)

⬇

Step 4: Deepen Understanding

Ask clarifying or detail questions. Paraphrase and summarize.

⬇

Step 5: Interact Through Questions

- Ask open-ended, mediating questions.
- Present theories (I wonder if _____ could be happening . . .).
- Make observations relating the coachees' exploration to what is known about the subject.

⬇

Step 6: Reflect and Brainstorm

- "What are you thinking now, given our conversation so far?"
- "Where in the situation do you see possibilities? What could you do?"

⬇

Step 7. Commit to Action

"What will you do between now and our next coaching conversation?"

Continue to the next coaching conversation beginning with Step 1.

Pacing the Steps in the Coaching Conversation

Most coaching conversations with a single client take between 50 and 75 minutes. Coaching conversations that involve two people or an entire team take longer and require different skills that merge group facilitation approaches to the coaching conversation frame. Working from timeframes of 50 and 75 minutes, Exhibit 4.2 depicts suggested pacing guides. Bear in mind that the pacing guides are *suggestions*. With experience, coaches detect the unique rhythm of each coachee and they become skilled in pacing each coaching conversation in service of their coachees.

 EXHIBIT 4.2   **Pacing Guide**

Step in the Coaching Conversation	If you have 50 minutes	If you have 75 minutes
Step 1: Greetings and Accountability	5 minutes	10 minutes
Step 2: Focus the Conversation	3 minutes	8 minutes
Step 3: Listen	10 minutes	12 minutes
Step 4: Deepen Understanding	10 minutes	12 minutes
Step 5: Interact Through Questions	15 minutes	20 minutes
Step 6: Reflect and Brainstorm	5 minutes	8 minutes
Step 7: Commit to Action	2 minutes	5 minutes

Details About Pacing the Coaching Conversation

Step 1: Greetings and Accountability. 5–10 minutes. This step involves some storytelling and catching up. Some coachees can pointedly summarize the events that transpired in the days between coaching sessions; others have a more meandering style. Although some venting is helpful, during this step, coaches should take note if most of the time is being used to vent, blame, or complain about who did what to vex the coachee. When coaches notice this happening, they can get the coachee back on track by saying something like, "I hear you've had a tough week! I wonder if you would summarize what you feel you were able to accomplish since our last coaching conversation."

Step 2: Focus the Conversation. 3–8 minutes. After coachees have a chance to hear themselves summarize what has taken place in the intervening time between coaching sessions, they often see pretty clearly what they need to focus this session on. In addition, well-crafted 100-day projects provide focused inspiration for what might need to be discussed in the current session.

Step 3: Listen. 10–12 minutes. Again, this is a storytelling step that reveals quite a bit about how coachees see their current reality. Coaches are highly "present" during this step, as demonstrated by listening. Coaches usually take copious notes during this step, even scripting almost everything the coachee says. Coaches do not ask questions or make comments during this time period. Even when the coachee pauses, the coach is careful not to butt in or move the coachee prematurely to step 4. Often, even after a pause that seems longer than comfortable, the coachee resumes the story. During this step, coachees commonly have pertinent insights as they hear themselves think out loud.

Step 4: Deepen Understanding. 10–12 minutes. As coaches ask their coachees for specific details or clarification of something that was said, they are beginning to draw attention to what seems to be important to pursue and further illuminate. Coaches may do several summaries or paraphrases during this step, but they most definitely end this step with a summary statement that invites the coachees to either correct the coach, or confirm that the coach understands the situation as the coachee sees the situation.

Step 5: Interact Through Questions. 15–20 minutes. The mediating and open-ended questions posed in step 5 encourage broad thinking around sometimes provocative ideas that jar the coachee into seeing perspectives of other people or considering new ideas that previously were unknowable or thought to be unrealistic. It can take a while to thoughtfully consider all that surfaces during this phase of the coaching session.

Step 6: Reflect and Brainstorm. 5–8 minutes. Step 6 is fueled by the energy generated in step 5. For this reason, coachees often have ideas about what they might do next on the tip of their tongues.

Step 7: Commit to Action. 2–5 minutes. By the time the coaching conversation reaches step 7, coachees are almost always ready to summarize the actions they have decided to commit to.

Chapter Summary

The coaching conversation process is a dynamic, yet structured, framework that draws coachees toward efficacy and confidence. Its elegant design creates space and time for crucial coaching strategies to be activated. Within the framework, coaches use the fundamental skills of listening, understanding, and asking mediating questions. In the next three chapters, we explore each of these skills in greater detail.

CHAPTER FIVE

Listening

BIG IDEAS IN CHAPTER FIVE

- ► Listening is the most important skill of coaches.
- ► To listen well, people have to break long-standing habits that prevent listening.
- ► Leaders who coach must be rigorous and attentive in developing their reputation for listening.
- ► Coaches choose to fall to silence and return to listening during the entire coaching conversation.

Listen

On the first day of my coach training workshops, I ask the class to engage in extended periods of time where they must simply listen to each other—a request that turns out to be more difficult than one might assume. I ask these coaches-in-training to identify a project that matters to them, pair up with a partner who may or may not be a complete stranger, and talk about it. Each person takes a turn, each round takes five minutes, and yes, I do use a stopwatch. Following in the steps of Paul Axtell, who first taught me how to coach, I provide the following rules: When in the coachee role, focus on a project that matters to you, speak about it for the entire time given (pauses are fine), and treat it like it matters. When in the coach role, do not inter-rupt, do not ask questions, do not comment, and treat it like it matters. It is the latter set of guidelines—the guidelines for when participants are in the coach role—that elicits groans of incredulity throughout the room. What? You mean coaches listen for five whole minutes before they get to say a word? Preposterous! How is that coaching?

But the progress made through coaching does not occur during the time the coach is speaking (Hargrove, 2007; Reeves and Allison, 2009 and 2010; Allison, 2010a). This point is made over and over again when I ask the coachees to raise their hands if they had a new insight or two about the issue they talked about while their partner coach was just listening. Invariably, hands shoot up throughout the room. At this point, I enjoy announcing with a bit of a flourish, "Ladies and gentlemen ... coaching!" Indeed, listening is so important to coaching that the desired outcome of coaching often begins long before coaches say a word.

What Stops People from Listening?

What makes the listening exercises in my coaching seminars so difficult is not that people are required to listen for five minutes without speaking, but that they have to stifle, at least for a while, the comfortable but unhelpful habits developed over the years that prevent them from really listening in the first place. These habits include the basics: interrupting, giving advice, not being able to resist sharing opinions, and taking over the conversation to make it about something that came to mind as the other person was speaking. Other unhelpful habits include needing to be right, multitasking, thinking about other things, and desperately needing to be known for having "marvelous" ideas. People in leadership positions might even fear that the people they lead will think them incompetent unless they interrupt with brilliant thoughts and opinions.

Habits are comfortable. Refraining from habits that prevent us from listening is quite uncomfortable. Some people squirm and find the pauses intolerable. As hard as it is to break the habits that prevent people from listening, make no mistake: Listening is the most important tool of great coaches.

What Listening Does for Coaches and for Coachees

A meta-analysis of the tools and skills used by coaches during coaching conversations reveals just how much listening matters, both to coaches and to coachees (Allison, 2010a).

When we listen, we show that we care. Some people even say that listening is a form of love. To not be listened to, claims Michael Nichols in his book *The Lost Art of Listening*, is "hard on the heart" (1995, p. 35). When I ask people in my workshops to talk about what people might think and feel when they have the impression they are being listened to, I hear responses that indicate that the person will think they are important, valued, and that their ideas matter. If you turn that same question around and ask what people might think and feel if they have the impression they are not being listened to, I hear opposite and bleak responses.

Toward the end of the first day of my coaching seminars, I give participants a homework assignment. I ask them to pay attention to how they listen to the people in their lives—family members, spouses, partners, coworkers, strangers, and their own children— outside of class, and come in the next morning prepared to share their stories. I'll never forget one woman who came to class on the second morning to tell us that she put aside all of her bad habits to "really listen" to her kindergartner the evening before. She described to the class how busy she usually is in the evening, making dinner, doing laundry, straightening up, checking in on her own mother by phone, and paying bills. This single mom decided to put it all aside and sit on a stool at her daughter's eye level and just listen as the little girl described her day. She told the class that it only took a few minutes, but the impact on her daughter was remarkable. The five-year-old talked for a while and then suddenly exclaimed, "Mommy, you really love me!" Yup, we all had lumps in our throats.

When coaches listen well, without judgment, resistance, or hubris, what transpires during the coaching session is relevant and compassionate. Coaches who listen with intention inspire trust. Within this trusting relationship, coachees share more details, say more about what they really think and feel, entertain more risks, and wrestle with tougher issues.

But the benefits of listening go way beyond the emotional value of building a trusting professional relationship. Listening is how coaches stay in the present moment, gathering critical data from which they will speak, when it is time for them to speak. Coaches who do not listen have no choice but to speak from their own experience, their own point of view, their own assumptions and biases.

Coaches who fail to listen at the start of the conversation, when their coachees declare what they want to focus their attention on and achieve by the end of the coaching session, deprive themselves of the very information they need to move the coaching session forward. How can a coach ask relevant and thought-provoking questions when they don't understand the issue at hand, and from the client's perspective? The coach who diminishes the value of listening is a coach who is not working in service of the coachee. Coaches who do not listen cannot speak or ask questions in service of their coachees and the goals they wish to achieve and that they asked to be coached on.

Listening and Leaders Who Coach

Leaders who coach their peers and the people they supervise are obliged to be even more rigorous about listening, especially when they are not in "coaching mode." For it is here, in the daily interactions of leaders, that reputations are built and reinforced. Leaders who are not good listeners when they supervise, advise, mentor, or teach the people who report to them will have a harder time stepping into a coaching role, no matter how much they might wish to do so (Allison, 2008).

In his book *Leading in a Culture of Change* (2001), Michael Fullan writes, "Beware of leaders who are always sure of themselves. Effective leaders listen attentively—you can almost hear them listening. Ineffective leaders make up their minds prematurely and, by definition, listen less thereafter" (pp. 123–124).

Listening, it turns out, is a leadership skill as much as it is a coaching skill. Dr. Lisa Sanders, author of *Every patient tells a story: Medical mysteries and the art of diagnosis* (2009), tells of two research studies that found that doctors allow patients to talk for an average of just 20 seconds before they interrupt. Some only allow three seconds. Moreover, the doctors in the study rarely if ever go back and ask the patient to finish what they were saying. The study found that when the doctors and patients are interviewed separately after the conversation, 50 percent of the time they disagree about the purpose of the visit.

Although Sanders writes specifically about the troublesome listening habits of physicians, many leaders in education frankly admit that they are known for giving answers, rendering judgments, and offering (in their most humble opinion) their point of view, which, nearly always, the person they are speaking to feels pressured or coerced to follow. To some leaders, giving answers *is* leadership. They fail to see the liabilities that come with having all the answers, all the time.

Fall to Silence

"Silence is a source of great strength."
LAO TZU

There is a Zen saying: "Do nothing." Like listening, "doing nothing" demands rigorous attention. To "do nothing," one has to overcome reactions and impulses. Instead of reacting, one must become very active, as the word "do" suggests, at, well, "nothing." The idea of "doing nothing" is strange and counterintuitive to most people—as strange as listening is in organizational cultures in which quick fixes and unfocused action are the norm. In daily conversations, people have strong urges to express themselves. They want to make points, be heard, convince others, and come across as clever and wise. These impulses make listening (really listening) counterintuitive.

Early in the coaching conversation, great coaches are deliberate about listening. After greeting the coachee and establishing the focus for the coaching session, a coach may listen for upwards of five to eight minutes before saying anything more than "Uh-huh," "I see," or "Tell me more." Novice coaches often find all of this listening unnerving. Inexperienced coaches often want to rush toward brainstorming about solutions to solve the problem, and they believe that they alone are responsible for making that happen. With experience and willingness to trust the process of coaching, novice coaches discover that answers cannot be forced, but must be uncovered and invented. Coachees need to hear their own thoughts; coaches must learn to fall to silence. Falling to silence is a lot like "doing nothing." To successfully fall to silence, coaches must choose to override impulses to hurry the coaching process toward premature conclusions (Allison, 2010a).

Listening to the coachee's current story is not only a specific "step" near the beginning of a coaching conversation, but it is an open tool for the entire coaching conversation. This means that when coaches ask questions or provide summaries, they must choose to then fall to silence so that coachees can reflect and respond. When coaches fall to silence, they give the coachees the time and space to work with the ideas that have come up. Coaches who do not fall to silence after speaking often find themselves delivering a minilecture on the ideas they embedded in the question they asked. This is a way of taking over the coaching conversation to make it about what they want to say rather than what the coachees need to think about in order to move their project forward.

Coaches do not mean to derail the coaching conversation by failing to fall to silence. Internally, they may be reacting to anxiety over the topic. Perhaps the issues hit close to home and remind them of something they, too, have wrestled with. Perhaps they "see" the answers clearly, and simply want to cut to the chase. While these impulses are well intended, they deprive the coachee of the process of coaching. With practice and awareness, coaches become aware of when they are not listening, and they choose to return to listening.

What Coaches "Do" When They Listen

Listening within the coaching conversation is a complex proposition. When coaches listen, they are not just hearing the words spoken by their coachees, but they are also operating on their own minds in at least two different ways.

Release Your Net of Memories

Coaches must facilitate real listening by noticing and letting go of their own inner chatter about what is being said. This is the chatter, loaded with judgments and resistance about what the coachee is saying, that flies around our minds. Things like, "That is the most ridiculous idea I've ever heard." Or, "Uh-oh, this coachee doesn't have a clue!" Or, "I don't see why that matters." Or, "That is not true at all." The ideas that coaches judge and resist are more relevant for them to explore with their own mentor than they are for sharing with coachees.

In fact, which ideas coaches judge and resist are determined by their own experiences. To express these ideas out loud would be destructive to the professional relationship between coaches and coachees and to the results sought by coachees. In his groundbreaking book on dialogue (1999), MIT lecturer William Isaacs writes, "To listen is to realize that much of our reaction to others comes from memory; it is stored reaction, not fresh response at all" (p.92). Isaacs says these memories predispose us to listen from a net of our own thoughts that we cast over the words we hear. When coaches remove the net of their own memories and listen to coachees with fresh minds, they successfully suspend the judgments and resistance that interferes with listening.

Sometimes what triggers the net of memories coaches cast over a conversation are the emotions expressed and displayed by coachees. Coaches naturally empathize with their coachees as they meet and wrestle with the inevitable antagonistic forces that come up in themselves and the organization. This empathy arises from the strong commitment coaches give to the project and outcomes sought by their coachees that undergirds the professional coaching relationship. In order to listen with intent, however, coaches must fortify themselves against becoming completely swamped by the emotions of their coachees. The International Coach Federation in part describes this as maintaining a coaching presence, character-ized by resistance to becoming overpowered and enmeshed by the emotions of coachees (2008). Great coaches monitor and self-regulate their emotions during coaching conversations so that they can be present and able to coach when the emotions of their coachees run high.

Listen on Behalf of the Coachee

The second way that coaches operate within their own minds to "do" listening is to track, prioritize, and intuit the importance of what coachees say, in relation to what coachees want to accomplish. These insights, intuitions, and prioritizations become visible in subsequent stages of the coaching conversation when coaches begin to make statements and ask questions. As they listen, coaches continuously consider and reconsider the relevance of each statement uttered by their coachees. In fact, during the first lab in my seminars, partici-pants inevitably tell me they were sorely tempted to interrupt and ask their coachees questions, only to learn moments later (because I impose the rule of listen, with no questions, interruptions, or com-ments) that what they intended to inquire about either came up nat-urally or was eventually deemed insignificant. In either case, they say they are grateful they were forced by the rules of the lab not to waste precious coaching time exploring something that mattered only incidentally to the coachee.

Thus, while listening, coaches hear the words of their coachees and recognize and release the net of their own memories that cause them to judge and resist what is being said, while simultaneously tracking and prioritizing important ideas in service of their coachees and what they wish to accomplish. If you did not believe that listening was difficult before now, you might now find the mere idea of listening—something you thought was as natural as breathing—daunting. But fear not: with mindfulness and intent, listening in this way becomes a way of being, especially when you decide to move into coaching mode.

This mindful approach to listening is treating the conversation and the person as if they matter. People who feel that they and their ideas matter see possibilities where previously none seemed to exist. They also see themselves as capable of much more than they originally allowed themselves to dream was possible.

Listening is the Gatekeeper to Great Coaching

Listening is a skill that everyone can improve. With practice, listening replaces habits of interrupting, giving advice, expressing opinions, and making conversations about ourselves. Great coaches understand that listening is the primary communication skill in their toolbox. Listening is the gatekeeper to the other powerful tools used by coaches, which include working with information to deepen understanding and asking questions that mediate and transform thinking.

In the next chapter, we will learn about the other powerful skills coaches use to support people. Those skills include asking clarifying and detail questions and providing summaries and paraphrases.

Deepening Understanding

BIG IDEAS IN CHAPTER SIX

► With deeper understanding, coachees begin to see their issues and concerns in a new light, or they see the "real issue."

► Understanding deepens when coachees respond to the detail and clarifying questions asked by coaches.

► Coaches demonstrate understanding by paraphrasing and summarizing what coachees have said.

► Coaches ask questions to deepen understanding and to position themselves to understand the most important aspects of a coachee's situation.

As presented in Chapter Four, the coaching conversation moves from an extended phase where coaches listen while coachees talk about what they are currently facing and what they wish to be coached on, to the next phase of the coaching conversation, in which coaches and coachees use specific communication skills to deepen mutual understanding. In step 4 of the coaching conversation, coaches use a set of three communication tools:

• Questions asked by the coach to clarify ambiguous or confusing parts of a coachee's story.

- Questions asked by the coach that seek relevant details of important topics raised by the coachee.
- Statements made by the coach that summarize, paraphrase, or translate what was said without changing the meaning and intention of the coachee.

The combined effect of asking clarifying questions, detail questions, and providing summaries and paraphrases is that coaches and coachees both understand the current situation and they provide each other with *assurances* that they understand each other. Coaches use this understanding to focus the next phases of the coaching conversation and to uncover nuances of the current situation of their coachees.

Deepening Understanding

Indeed, within the context of coaching, "understanding" is more than making sure everyone is on the same page. For starters, the paraphrases, summaries, and clarifying and detail questions expressed by the coach lead the coachee to focus on what *might* matter most. For coaches, how coachees respond to the inquiries put forth provides essential data about the current situation that allow the coach to mindfully select their next coaching move. This matters because the last thing someone in "coaching mode" wants to do is ask irrelevant questions or make distracting comments that lead others down a path that is out of sync with the wisdom they possess. After all, empowering others to inspired action is the primary goal of coaching.

Questions to Clarify and Ask for Details

The following are examples of clarifying and detail questions asked by educational coaches of their coachees:

- "When you said 'team leader,' do you mean team leaders for each grade range, or team leaders for each subject area?"

- "Could you clarify what you mean when you say 'new teachers'? Are these teachers who are new to teaching or new to your system?"
- "Can you give me an example of what you mean when you say the system itself is resistant?"
- "Tell me more about the details of the feedback you would like from the team."

Clarifying and detail questions reduce ambiguity and increase specificity. As coachees hear themselves respond to the questions coaches ask that beg for clarity and detail, they begin to see, hear, and understand their own "take" on the situation, perhaps for the first time. We all feel that we know and understand our own situations. When it comes to complex matters, however, we often have an incorrect impression of our own thoughts about the matter, but we don't realize it until we hear ourselves describe it out loud to someone who listens in a way that facilitates this awareness.

When coachees tell the story of their current situation, they cover a lot of territory. They often refer to many ideas, shift between topics, go off on tangents into stories that cause them to lose track of their points, and make vague references to an assortment of people, processes, and desired outcomes. In response to being bombarded with all of this information, coaches certainly ask clarifying questions so that they come to better understand the coachee's situation. But coaches also ask clarifying questions when they completely understand the ideas expressed, but they believe their coachees will benefit from hearing themselves elaborate and illuminate the ideas and references that seem to be at the heart of what they desire and seek.

Here are examples of sentence stems that begin questions coaches use to ask for clarification and details (Allison, 2010a):

- Are you saying X or Y?
- Can you clarify this?

- Can you give an example of this?

- Can you give me details about...?

- Say more about...

- What do you mean?

Summarizing and Paraphrasing Statements

Statements made by coaches to summarize and paraphrase the accounts of their coachees have multiple functions. First, they convey to coachees that the coach has tracked and understood the most important ideas in the story. Second, summaries and paraphrases serve as questions that invite elaboration, clarification, and details. For example, if a coach offers a paraphrase such as "You are drawn to option B for the following reasons ... " the coachee is likely to provide additional information. Third, summarizing and paraphrasing statements frame the essential dilemmas, options, or viewpoints through the eyes of the coachee. For example, a coach could summarize an account provided by the coachee by saying, "It appears that you have three priorities—A, B, and C—and they each require different resources." Fourth, what coaches select to paraphrase and summarize draws the attention of their coachees to those matters. This conveys insight for the coachee about what the coach discerns as important, based on the full context of the coachee's situation.

Here are examples of sentence stems that begin the summary and paraphrase statements made by coaches in step 4 of the coaching conversation (Allison, 2010a):

- So...

- In other words...

- You're saying that...

- There seem to be two issues here...

- You're concerned about...

- You're seeing...

The Coaching Conversation in Step 4

As has been said earlier in this book, coaching is both an art and a science. As a science, coaches make explicit use of the coaching conversation phases with the knowledge that it will lead their coachees toward understanding and action. For example, in the early phases of the coaching conversation, coachees state what they want to be coached on and what they want to accomplish by the end of the coaching conversation. What coachees say they want to focus on alerts coaches about what to specifically listen for and ask questions about. As an art, coaches develop the knack for knowing just what parts of the conversation to linger on, clarify, and elaborate so that coachees are likely to have insights about the ideas that are most relevant.

Here is a sample coaching conversation (adapted from Allison, 2010a) that illustrates a coach artfully using the science of the coaching conversation and asking clarifying questions and detail questions, and offering summaries and paraphrases:

> COACH: "Mary, it's great to be with you for this coaching session. Tell me how the actions you committed to at the end of our last coaching session went and where you are now in your project."

> MARY: "Well, as you know, I made the decision at the end of our last coaching conversation to gather together the four lead teachers of the core content areas to tell them for the first time about my vision of adding a data analysis process to the Professional Learning Community meetings. I have to say, it went really well considering that this additional process will surely rock a few boats in the teaching ranks when we begin to share the idea with the rest of the faculty. The lead teachers agree this is a necessary step and they also agree to help me plan the rest of the project. After we talked about it, we decided the project is now at a point where it needs at least one team to willingly try the process and give

us some feedback on what worked well and where the hiccups occurred. So, I'd like to use this coaching session to think through how to get one teacher team to buy into the idea and use the process for the next nine weeks. I think I want them to share their experience with the rest of the faculty at the meeting next week. Of course, I'm hoping it will go well, so the rest of the faculty is easily convinced!"

COACH: "Mary, let me summarize what I've heard so far. First, the four lead teachers gave you their support, and as a group, you decided that the next step is to recruit a willing team to give the process a go, provide you and the four lead teachers with feedback, and share their experience with the faculty next week." *(summary)*

MARY: "Yes, exactly. I'm really thrilled with the momentum we have at this point. And I think we have a team or two to choose from to pilot the process. I would hate to lose this opportunity to gain early feedback about how the process works in a real team of teachers."

COACH: "Momentum gives you a sense of energy. You sound like you want to strike while the iron is hot, as they say!" *(metaphor, paraphrase)*

MARY: "I do. See, just one or two teachers have a way of taking the wind out of the sails of every initiative, no matter how much the research supports it. I don't want them convincing the other teachers that the process is a bad one before we even have a chance to see how it works for a real team."

COACH: "Mary, I'd like to ask a clarifying question. When you say you want to pilot the process with a willing team, do you mean a team that does not have members who shoot down initiatives no matter what they are?" *(clarifying question)*

MARY: "Yes, that is definitely part of what I'm looking for, but I also want a team that 'gets it.' A team that understands how implementing common strategies and reflecting on their impact will make them better teachers. I want a team that is eager to learn."

COACH: "So you're looking for a pilot team eager to implement common strategies because it will make them better teachers. Mary, tell me more about what you want the pilot team to give you and the four team leaders feedback on. Do you have some specific points in mind?" *(summary and detail question)*

MARY: "Yes, I do have some ideas about the feedback we need, as a matter of fact, but I haven't had a chance to think them all the way through. Up to this point, I've been thinking mostly about the process itself and the amount of time each step takes and how that works for them in the 45-minute block available."

The above exchange between Mary and her coach illustrates the communication skills characteristic of step 4. Notice that the coach discerns important ideas, brings them forward, and then adds the question or summary statements to expand and deepen understanding.

The Importance of Deepening Understanding

If coaches neglect to master the communication skills required in this phase of coaching, the rest of the conversation will feel off-kilter, to both the coach and the coachee. The same is true if either party rushes this phase of the conversation. Without thorough understanding of the coachee's perspective, coaches ask questions that are off-track and irrelevant. What other choice do they have? If coaches do not truly understand the coachee's situation, through the eyes of the coachee, the questions can only come from either a vague understanding of the situation, or from the coach's own point of view. Off-kilter questions make the coachee feel that the coach must have thrown a dart at a list of possible coaching questions and asked the one that the dart pierced. Alternatively, coaches ask relevant and focused questions when they have spent ample time in step 4, offering several summaries and paraphrases, asking focused detail and clarifying questions, and listening deeply to how their coachees respond to each.

Step 4 Pitfalls

While in step 4 of the coaching conversation, in which coaches and coachees seek to deepen understanding, coaches must avoid two common pitfalls when it comes to asking questions: asking for details or clarification out of a voyeuristic need to know, and asking questions based on their past experiences and interests instead of from the contexts of their coachees' current situations.

The first pitfall, asking details out of a personal need to know, may be the result of bad habits developed over a lifetime of interacting with others without mindful intention about how to use conversations to be supportive and inspiring. Leaders who find themselves with a coach who asks questions that are not helpful to them or their situation may be working with a person who lacks the ability to maintain their coaching presence and role when the topic reminds them of their own work and life. Coaches who lose their coaching presence succumb to internal reactions that come up for them as they engage with coachees and listen to their stories (O'Neill, 2000). Undisciplined or untrained coaches fall easily out of the coaching role. I remember hearing a person talk about "coaching" another person who worked in a school district in which the superintendent announced his retirement. The "coach" confided she was calling her coachee more frequently out of an insatiable desire to hear gossip about her coachee's school district. This scenario provides a gross (and I do mean disgusting in addition to extreme) example of an unskilled and unhelpful coach who abused the privilege of coaching in order to satisfy her personal need. Leaders who want to work with a coach should avoid internal or external coaches who gossip, especially when they do so during coaching engagements. Coaches who gossip *with* their coachees, gossip *about* their coachees.

The second pitfall, when coaches ask questions driven by focusing on their previous experiences and not the current situation of their coachees, is less sinister in motive than the first pitfall, but has a negative impact on coaching all the same.

Coaches who ask questions that reflect their experience are making at least two unhelpful assumptions. First, they are assuming that the current situations of their coachees are identical to situations they experienced. This, of course, is never true. No matter how effective coaches were or are in educational leadership roles similar to their coachees', the milieu is completely different for their coachees. The people are different, the decisions are different, the data are different, the climates are different, and the roles their coachees have within the culture of their organizations and the people they interact with are different. To be helpful, coaching questions must always be relative to coachees' situations (Braun, 2009).

The second assumption being made when coaches ask questions that are not relative to the context of their coachees is that the coach knows better than the coachee about what to do, and the coachee should, in fact, do what the coach would do. This assumption flies in the face of the purpose of coaching. Coaching is a process for drawing out the wisdom of coachees so they not only accomplish important work but also deepen their capacity to accomplish great work. Coaches who tell their coachees what to do short-circuit the process of learning and diminish the returns that coaching makes possible.

The Ladder of Inference

I once saw a bumper sticker that said, "Your head is like a bad neighborhood. Don't go there alone." I find this quote charming for this simple reason: it is *so* true. Left to our own devices, we can innocently interpret visible data inaccurately and either make mountains out of molehills or lemonade out of rotten lemons. Leaders who ask for coaching must understand at some level that they think better in the company of a coach. Coaches use clarifying questions and detail questions and provide summaries and paraphrases to mitigate the faulty conclusions that even highly effective leaders draw from time to time when they are left to explore the contents of their minds alone.

Organizational learning guru Chris Argyris (1993) invented a model that helps us understand the cognitive activity of our minds whenever we experience anything in the physical world. He calls it the Ladder of Inference because it reveals how the human mind causes us to rapidly arrive at decisions about what to do (actions to take) as if we were climbing up the rungs of a ladder. The Ladder of Inference is a useful mental model for coaches to use to further focus the questions they ask in step 4 of the coaching conversation.

As can be seen in Exhibit 6.1, the Ladder of Inference begins with witnessable data that is visible to others. Witnessable data occurs in the physical world and is visible to all who care to look at it. As soon as people witness data, however, they draw only what they choose to pay attention to into their minds, where they rapidly work with it, out of sight of others and often even of themselves. This is where assumptions that often lead to unhelpful actions begin. Still invisible to others, the individual quickly leaps from paying attention only to the data they select to adding meaning and making assumptions. What they assume to be true then turns into conclusions about the data they selected and then into firm beliefs. Out of beliefs come actions which occur in plain sight of others again, becoming visible data themselves. When the actions of one person are based on the

EXHIBIT 6.1   **The Ladder of Inference**

I take actions: Visible to others

5. I adopt beliefs

4. I draw conclusions

3. I make assumptions

2. I add meaning

1. I select data to pay attention to

Witnessable data: Visible to others

Source: Adapted from Argyris (1993)

data they selected to pay attention to, which differs from the data that another person selects to pay attention to (and draws conclusions from), both parties scratch their heads in confusion.

Coaches who reference the Ladder of Inference in step 4 of the coaching conversation help their coachees better understand how they and others arrived at decisions and actions. Here are some examples of questions educational coaches ask in step 4 when the Ladder of Inference is in play:

- "Tell me more about the data you focused on as you selected the strategies for your school." (*detail question about the data selected*)

- "Can you clarify what you mean when you say that the superintendent obviously means to exclude your school from the grant?" (*clarifying question about the meaning added to the data in the mind of the coachee*)

- "So you believe that the Data Teams value the time provided to meet because they never fail to gather together on Thursday afternoons." (*summary statement about what the coachee believes to be true*).

The field of organizational learning provides a variety of mental models that are infinitely helpful to coaches. The Ladder of Inference is just one of many, but it is extremely powerful and applicable in step 4 of the coaching conversation.

Readiness for Step 5

The minds of coaches actively seek to make sense of the stories told by their coachees. Coaches who rush step 4 of the coaching conversation deprive themselves of the information and insight they need to appropriately summarize and paraphrase the coachees descriptions and ask helpful clarifying and detail questions. This has a negative ripple effect on the rest of the coaching process, for if understanding is not achieved in step 4, coaches cannot ask mediating questions in service of coachees and their projects in step 5, which we explore in detail in the next chapter.

Fresh Thinking— Asking Mediating Questions

BIG IDEAS IN CHAPTER SEVEN

► Coaches who ask mediating questions resist giving advice and making recommendations.

► Mediating questions require exploration more than "answers."

► Mediating questions are open-ended and facilitate new insights, ideas, perspectives, and options.

► Coaches ask mediating questions to focus their coachee's attention on what the coachee wishes to achieve.

► Mediating questions cause coachees to "own" their ideas, co-create with the coach, and reflect on meanings.

► Mediating questions can be provocative because they stretch thinking.

During step 5 of the coaching conversation, coaches ask questions that go beyond the information shared by coachees during previous steps of the coaching conversation. These questions are less to be "answered" by coachees than they are to be explored, pondered, and illuminated (Allison, 2010a). Coaches must bear in mind that everything they ask and say in the coaching conversation draws their coachee's focus. Knowing this, great coaches ask questions that focus coachees on expanding their thoughts, in service of what *coachees* wish to accomplish. Great coaches recognize the responsibility they have to their coachees to ask questions that aid them in accomplishing their important work. Great coaches are careful not to diminish their coachees' ability to focus on what matters most to them.

Mediating Questions

Mediating questions help people connect to information in a way that helps them understand themselves, others, and the larger context of their situation while they simultaneously think about the meaning of it all (Costa and Garmston, 1994). They are open-ended and devoid of judgment; they do not imply that the coach knows the "right" answer. Mediating questions draw out tacit wisdom in coachees. For coaches, asking mediating questions suspends the impulse to provide solutions and offer advice (Hargrove, 2007).

When coaches ask mediating questions, they move from working with coachees on ideas already in play to ideas that may become possible (Adams, 2009). In the course of coaching conversations, mediating questions have at least three dynamic effects on coachees:

1. Coaches cannot predict how their coachees will respond and engage with the mediating questions they pose to them. Therefore, coachees "own" the insights that begin to surface and they begin to take responsibility for the actions that come from those insights.

2. Mediating questions provide coachees with an initial framework on which they can build ideas. This results in the co-creation of insights and solutions while coaches stay in service of their coachees.

3. Mediating questions press for reflection, which provides coachees with *time* to think differently, understand their thoughts better, and discover how to express them to others.

Coaches must avoid asking questions that manipulate the coachee to come to a point of view that the coach feels is the "right" answer. Great coaches respect the goals and focus of their coachees. They listen in order to determine the best questions to inspire coachees further toward their desires, not to steer them in the direction of preconceived outcomes more reflective of the coaches' anxieties.

Mediating Questions Ask Much of Coachees

Coaches often ask provocative mediating questions that ask coachees to explore research and concepts related to the issue at hand (Marquardt, 2005). I call these "thought leadership coaching questions" (Allison, 2010a). Thought leadership coaching questions adhere to the purpose of coaching, which is to mediate extraordinary thinking in others, but they also introduce theories and research that expand coachees' thinking. Consider these examples of specific thought leadership coaching questions:

- "How does the team feel about increasing collaborative lesson planning?"
- "How do effective teaching strategies fit into these school-wide changes?"
- "How do the people who report to you respond when you ask them for data about their effectiveness? What is your level of confidence that they can obtain the data they need to communicate with you?"
- "How do the standards for administrators shape the current evaluation system?"

These demanding questions retain the qualities we see in well-crafted open-ended questions while simultaneously focusing coachees on important ideas in teaching, learning, and leadership. They are open-ended to encourage inquiry as opposed to a "right" answer, they are within the context of the coachee's concern, and they cause the coachee to draw on and reflect upon their experiences and extend them within the current scenario (Stoltzfus, 2008; Exhibit 7.1).

Coaching Scenario: Oscar

Oscar is a first-year junior high principal working with two assistant principals who are also in their first year on the job. During one of his coaching conversations, Oscar told his coach that his priority was to instill a sense of order in the school; to make it a safe and orderly place where teachers can teach and students can learn. The indicator that Oscar identified to monitor is the number of classroom referrals to the main office for disciplinary problems. Oscar said his goal is to reduce the number of referrals by 50 percent by the end of the school year. To accomplish this goal, Oscar told his coach that he planned to ask the guidance counselor to conduct a work-

 EXHIBIT 7.1 Essential Characteristics of Mediating Questions

- Open-ended: require a longer individualized response, such as, "What would you like to accomplish this year?"

- Place coachees and their context at the heart of the question: "How has your perspective evolved with the new data?"

- Provocative: excite and stimulate the conversation, such as, "What would happen if...." Provocative questions ask coachees to consider something more, less, or different.

- Evocative: pull coachees into their issues and bring emotional energy to mind, such as, "What makes you feel most engaged with your faculty?"

shop about a classroom discipline program for the whole staff on the first institute day in August.

Spend a few minutes thinking about Oscar's situation as he explained it to his coach. Consider these three questions:

1. What are your observations about Oscar's plan so far?

2. What do you discern to be the most important ideas in Oscar's plan?

3. What mediating questions would you ask Oscar in step 5 of the coaching conversation?

The framework formed by the questions above encourages Oscar's coach to ask mediating questions that are helpful to Oscar. Let's examine the thought process of a coach using the three-question framework.

During step 5 of the coaching conversation, coaches first seek clarity about the important ideas in their coachee's story as they relate to the goals of the coachee. For example, Oscar clearly states that he wants the guidance counselor at his middle school to conduct a workshop about a classroom discipline program for the whole staff on the first institute day in August. Therefore, in response to the first question in the framework, Oscar's coach would note the following observations:

- Oscar is a first-year principal and both his assistant principals are new as well.

- Oscar has made a decision to focus on classroom discipline.

- Oscar has a goal to reduce classroom referrals by 50 percent.

- Oscar wants his guidance counselor to take the lead.

Out of these observations, Oscar's coach might highlight the following important ideas (the second question in the framework):

Important Idea 1: Oscar sees his guidance counselor as capable of taking the lead on this project, yet he does not mention his role in the workshop or the roles of his two assistant principals.

Important Idea 2: Oscar uses data and sets clear goals.

Important Idea 3: Oscar sees the classroom management program as important for the entire faculty.

Important Idea 4. Oscar wants to start the year off with a classroom management strategy in place.

Important Idea 5: Oscar wants a safe and orderly school.

Out of the ideas that the coach deems important (and checks for accuracy through summaries and paraphrases that the coachee confirms or revises for the coach) come the mediating questions (which are focused on Oscar's stated goal) that the coach will finally ask. Here are some examples of mediating questions that Oscar's coach might ask him:

1. "Oscar, talk about the roles of everyone you see involved with implementing the classroom management program after the workshop in August."

2. "Oscar, your confidence in the counselor is strong. How will that person make the workshop a winning event?"

3. "Where are the nuances in the data? Where do you see strengths and challenges in student behavior?"

4. "Oscar, how do you view the connections between classroom management and a safe and orderly school-wide environment?"

Oscar's coach would be out of line to ask leading questions to discourage Oscar from asking his guidance counselor to hold the classroom management workshop in August, even if the coach disagreed with Oscar's plan. Leading questions are questions that have the ulterior motive of trying to make coachees respond in a way that the coach finds satisfying (Marquardt, 2005). We would not want to hear Oscar's coach asking him disingenuous questions such as, "Are you sure you want your guidance counselor to do the workshop?" Or, "Usually August is a bad time for workshops like this, what do you think?" A great coach would ask Oscar mediating questions in service of his goal that also allow him to probe his own mind for both rational and intuitive insight. As Oscar wrestles with well-crafted mediating questions, he will discover insights, and understand their meaning relative to his work and his leadership responsibilities.

The Right Question

People who are new to coaching often find it challenging to ask mediating questions that are both effective and strengthen the relationship with their coachees. Initially, they believe there is a "right" question and they are concerned they will not know what it is or know how to ask it. The truth is, an algorithm does not exist for matching a question perfectly to every situation. Instead, through thoughtful trial and error, the coach becomes adept at asking the right question at the right time. Do not struggle to ask the "right" questions. If you do not know what to ask, go back to eliciting additional important information from your coachee with a question that begins with the opener, "Tell me more about…" And then, just listen.

Sample Mediating Question Openers

Here are sample openers to mediating questions (Allison, 2010a). These openers may inspire helpful mediating questions.

- Who else has an interest in how this turns out?
- What person or network has a piece of this puzzle?
- What don't you know about this issue, and who does know those things?

- What are you "sure of?" Is that preventing you from seeing another point of view?
- Who agrees with you? Who disagrees with you?
- What do you need to communicate and to what person or network?
- What could you learn from the opposite point of view? What person or network has strong opinions about this issue?
- What follow-up needs to take place?
- What might motivate people to participate?
- What seems to be the main obstacle to your vision?
- If you could wipe the slate clean, what would you do?
- What obstacles might have to be removed?
- What are you not getting to?
- What requests could you make to move this forward?
- What relationship or conversation is missing?
- What do you feel like doing?
- What do you need to get scheduled?
- What do you need to ask someone else to do for you?
- What do you need to communicate?
- What should you decide not to do and take off your list?
- What do you need to stop in order to make room for something else?
- What do you need to get started on?
- What do you and others need to learn?

PART 3

The Coaching Project

Selecting Coaching Projects

BIG IDEAS IN CHAPTER EIGHT

► Projects give coaching focus, creating value and interest for coaches and coachees.

► Coaching projects provide a context for leadership growth.

► Learning gained in coaching projects is transferred to other projects.

► Leaders serve the goals and mission of the organization through the projects they take responsibility for.

► Leaders use coaching to advance the most important work they do.

Some leaders balk at setting up one project in order to focus the coaching. "But I have 20 important projects on my plate!" they cry. These leaders often want to persuade the person who agrees to coach them to simply leave each coaching conversation open to talk about whatever comes up—whatever seems most pressing at the moment. The "let's not have a project" approach is a sure way to seriously undermine one of the most powerful outcomes of coaching: accomplishing something important to improve the organization (Reeves and Allison, 2009). Getting better at doing one project exceptionally well does not make your other projects worse. It is not a zero-sum game. Although focusing your coaching conversations on one important project when you have 20 on your plate and are in the midst of putting out fires may feel counterintuitive at first, the learning that occurs within this one project has a ripple effect on other important projects (Goldsmith & Reiter, 2007).

The Importance of Projects to Coaching

Without a project, coaching becomes a series of unrelated chats that rarely lead to visible outcomes. Lacking a project to focus the coaching, both coaches and coachees begin to doubt that coaching has value. Coachees become bored and lose their enthusiasm for coaching, causing them to miss previously scheduled sessions. Without a project, coachees lack context for growing in leadership. Moreover, the gains expected from coaching for the organization vanish, and coaching becomes simply another good idea that did not work out.

Coach-Worthy Projects

Coaching is an expensive proposition if leaders only want to be coached on tasks that do not create value by contributing to the mission of the organization (Allison, 2010a). Leaders who understand the power of coaching want to be coached on projects for which coaching will provide an advantage and projects that could suffer or even fail if coaching were not available. Coach-worthy projects possess qualities that add value to the organization. Specifically, they:

1. Are visible and tangible; something new or different in the system. People can point to them, speak about them, monitor their progress and impact, and "tell the story" about how they came into being. Examples are new programs, approaches, practices, and structures.

2. Show clear value toward moving the mission of the organization forward. Projects are how leaders get things done (Kouzes and Pozner, 2003). Therefore, projects always align to organizational goals (often at multiple levels within the system, as well as multiple goals) and implement the strategies of the organization. Consider this example and notice the cascading progression down to where the rubber meets the road, which is this principal's project that could benefit from coaching:

- **District Mission:** To create opportunities for all students to learn and succeed at high levels.

- **District Goal:** To reduce the achievement gap between all students and African American students.

- **District Strategy:** Improve the district reading, writing, and speaking literacy program in the middle schools.

- **Individual Principal's Project:** Implement writing across the curriculum and score student work using a common rubric.

3. Are consistent with the role of the leader who is being coached. The leader's coaching project must be appropriate to the leader's role and fall into the leader's circle of influence and control. Coachees must be empowered to take action within their project either with others or through others. Other leaders may be working on projects through their positions to contribute to the accomplishment of the same goal.

4. Can be monitored for implementation and effectiveness over the **short term.** Leaders monitor project implementation indicators and project impact indicators. Project implementation indicators show that the project itself is moving forward. Examples of this are:

- The number of professional development sessions on writing and using rubrics offered to elementary classroom teachers.

- The percentage of classroom teachers who identify themselves as literacy teachers.

- The schedule that contains common teacher planning time for evaluating student writing.

- The percentage of teachers trained in using the writing rubric.

- The percentage of teachers using the rubric to provide students with feedback about their writing in each grade level.

- The percentage of students using the rubric to self-evaluate.

- The percentage of students who write at least one five-paragraph essay every week.

- The percentage of students whose writing has increased in proficiency as measured by the rubric.

5. Can be evaluated for implementation and effectiveness over the **long term.** Because projects "roll out" district strategies and goals, their impact can be judged over the long term by trends in organizational data. For instance, in the example presented above in which a principal's project is to implement writing across the curriculum as part of a strategy to improve the literacy program in the district so that more African American students achieve at high levels, then some of the indicators the principal could monitor include:

- The percentage of African American students who are proficient or better in each academic subject as measured by state end-of-year assessments.

- The percentage of African American students

enrolled in Advance Placement courses in high school.

- The percentage of African American students who pass all portions of the graduation requirement tests and graduate and go on to post-secondary education centers.

6. Have a beginning, middle, and end. Projects have a start date and a due date. In between are ranges when certain milestones are met that demonstrate the project is moving forward.

7. Require the involvement of other people in the system to help launch, implement, support, and evaluate the project.

Keep it Simple

Projects are complex enough. Coming up with a coaching project should not be a complicated ordeal, nor should it require strict protocols for how projects are identified and declared. When it is difficult for leaders to identify projects they could be coached on, I have greater concerns about the focus and purpose of the organization. I once saw a whole group of leaders reject coaching because they did not want to have to "come up" with a project. The fact is, projects *are* the work.

Projects are the way leaders accomplish things. Except in educational organizations that lack focused vision, myriad projects worthy of and ripe for coaching already sit on the plates of every leader. Consider the scenario of Brian, a first-year assistant superintendent for curriculum. How many projects do you detect in Brian's situation?

Brian's predecessor believed that kids are over-assessed these days. As a result of that belief, his district never created a framework for formative assessment. Brian's district has only the state assessment to analyze for feedback about how effective they are as a public school district. Everyone in the district realizes that the feedback from the state assessment paints an incomplete picture, is untimely, and provides only summative results. Some teachers, parents, and administrators have been asking for evidence that students are learning throughout the year. Teachers do not want to spend a lot more time assessing students, however, if the results are not easy to obtain and cannot be used immediately to improve instruction.

Most people who read this scenario immediately identify a number of coach-worthy projects for Brian, everything from designing a system for formative assessment to establishing a data repository and system for analyzing data and revising curriculum and instruction based on decisions made from linking formative and summative assessments to classroom practices.

Real Leaders, Real Projects

Here are examples of some of the projects I have personally had the privilege to coach leaders on:

- A human resources director asked me to coach her as she developed a new teacher induction program that required new teachers to work with a mentor on an action research project.
- A principal asked to be coached as he developed teacher leaders to coach teachers who were differentiating units of instruction to better serve their students in special education.
- An academic coach asked to be coached as she created the implementation program for a new curriculum map and textbook adoption.
- A technology specialist asked to be coached as he developed a district-wide data repository and analysis system.

- A superintendent asked to be coached on realigning the principal's evaluation program to state and national standards.

- A superintendent asked to be coached on instituting a structure, process, and practice for school-level administrators to report student success indicators and strategies at one leadership meeting per month.

What projects could you be coached on to improve the work you are responsible for in your organization? Exhibit 8.1 provides a simple protocol for exploring your options.

Giving and Receiving Coaching

The projects on the plate of any leader in any educational organization at any given moment are usually large, complex, messy, and involve many other people. They are also important and truly are the work of the organization. Any one of them would provide a great opportunity for coaching to make a difference. When coaching is combined with a project that matters, the return compounds. This is because not only do coachees accomplish work that matters, but

 EXHIBIT 8.1 Exploring Coaching Options

A Simple Conversation to Define the Coaching Project

What are the leadership decisions, projects, or initiatives you are responsible for this year or have identified for yourself this year?

Which one do you feel passion for?

Which one could make the greatest difference for the mission of your school/district/organization?

Would you like to be coached on that?

they also deepen their capacity, through coaching, to do more work that matters, and do it better.

Imagine what could happen in your organization if more leaders engaged in coaching, both providing coaching to peers and colleagues, and asking for coaching on their most important projects. If you are working with a coach now, make sure that you are receiving coaching on a project that can make a difference. If you see a peer or colleague doing work that matters, ask them if you can coach them.

The next chapter provides practical information and steps for creating a usable 100-day project.

Setting Up the 100-Day Project

BIG IDEAS IN CHAPTER NINE

► 100-day projects can make initiatives successful during the launching and implementation phases.

► The 100-day project is a practical project management tool that shows what a leader intends to do to initiate a project.

► Project strategies match the context and culture of the educational system.

► High-impact actions taken in the first 100 days of a project create momentum and the opportunity to refine processes.

► High-impact actions involve learning, looking at evidence, considering people and attitudes, and making decisions.

Educational leaders are often surprised to learn that certain actions taken in the first 100 days of launching initiatives can create success for the project during the implementation phase as well (Watkins, 2003). Earlier chapters of this book established the fact that coaching done well increases leadership effectiveness. Chapter Eight focused on the importance of projects and explained how to identify a project for coaching. This chapter illuminates how to use 100-day project planning to launch the projects that leaders bring to coaching.

100 Days

The 100-day project is a plan that declares high-impact actions to launch a leadership project and create early wins within 100 days (Reeves and Allison, 2009 and 2010). The 100-day project provides a system that helps educational leaders to think in advance about the actions they need to take to get their project underway. When the 100-day project is combined with coaching, leaders have an extra advantage: they have a coach who will skillfully create conversations for the leader to think through each action and reflect on its impact. Through these coaching conversations, leaders have time and energy to understand their plans, develop effective and innovative ideas, consider ways to enhance their success, and reflect and learn from whatever happens.

What the 100-Day Project Is and Is Not

The 100-day project, as described in Chapter Eight, focuses the coaching conversations between leaders and their coaches. It is a simple project management system that shows what a leader intends to do in the first 100 days of either beginning a new project or revitalizing an existing project.

As can be seen in Exhibit 9.1, the 100-day project is an adaptive project management tool that provides leaders and their coaches with a single location for planning actions and reflecting on the impact of those actions. To be of value, the 100-day project must align with the mission and goals of the organization. To be valuable to the leader, it must be practical, personal, and mutable in order to reflect the changing needs of the organization as the project unfolds (Allison, 2010a).

What the 100-Day Project Is and Is Not

The 100-day project is...	The 100-day project is not...
A call for action over inaction to produce early results that suggest how to revise and respond.	A useless exercise in writing yet another plan that has little impact on the real work of leaders.
A "living" project management tool. The 100-day plan is not written in stone. In fact, coachees will revise it as needed, at the end of coaching sessions.	Put in a file after it is written or tossed into the trash once the project is executed.
An action that clearly aligns with the mission of the organization.	Based on goals and strategies different from the coachee's organization. Leaders already have many important projects on their plate that they need to start or revitalize, and should pick one they feel passionate about.
A single place where leaders personally record and track the actions they plan to take to move their project forward.	An accountability document written to comply with mandates.
A starting point for every coaching conversation.	A plan submitted to the coach, never to be consulted and revised.
A learning journal that captures and holds historical information about what it took to implement the project.	An exercise that reduces the time available for learning and reflection.

Exhibit 9.2 depicts a sample 100-day project. This sample is the project of a high school principal who wants to build teacher leadership through action research about school-wide practices to positively impact student learning in language arts and math classes. His project involves finding teacher leaders who would like to learn and use the process of action research in order to make recommen-

Sample 100-Day Project

Project Title: "Teacher Leadership Through Action Research"

Date	Actions
6/27/09	Share my vision of how action research develops teacher leaders. Obtain feedback via a survey done in the staff meeting.
6/27/09	Start 100-day leadership plan.
6/30/09	Look at student achievement data and establish baseline scores.
7/3/09	Invite volunteer teachers to team up and become the first to do action research on one of the three strategies: grading, teacher assignment, and common formative assessment.
7/7/09	Provide professional development on how to conduct action research.
7/14/09	Teams schedule the events of their project.
7/14/09	Teams develop their agreements and protocols for their project.
7/17/09	Teams prepare project progress presentation for stakeholders.
7/22/09	Analyze policies and procedures that affect all three areas.
7/28/09	Distribute findings and refer again to the vision that paints a picture of hope.
8/4/09	Teams begin the action research project. Identify research questions and methods.
8/7/09	Hold support and feedback meeting for teams.
8/13/09	Identify milestones for tracking small wins.
9/1/09	Visit classrooms as projects begin. Begin to collect impact stories as students respond.
9/4/09	Strategy teams check in and midcourse corrections are made.
9/7/09	Update superintendent and senior leadership team.
9/11/09	Second presentation is given by action research teams, focused on evidence of student learning, engagement, and faculty morale.
9/15/09	Teams meet to refine procedures and protocols.
9/18/09	Second assessment of student learning in targeted areas is administered.
9/22/09	Data are analyzed, with a focus on evidence of student learning, engagement, and faculty morale.
9/27/09	Technology support person conducts a comparative analysis looking at student achievement, engagement, and morale in the classes that did not use the strategies.
10/1/09	Action research teams meet to analyze and interpret the data.
10/3/09	Announce with complete transparency what worked, what failed, what we learned, how next semester will be different, and what we can apply now on a school-wide or system-wide basis.
10/6/09	Hold a debriefing with the core action research teams about lessons learned, including feedback on the impact and the process.

dations about how to improve teacher assignment, grading, and common formative assessment. In addition, this principal identified two areas where he wanted to improve as a leader: sharing the vision and following up on details.

Notice that this plan contains just 24 high-impact actions, all of them written at a macro level of detail. Clearly, the 100-day project is not a tome. Nor is it a tedious task analysis of each and every step that this principal will need to take during the course of the project. What the 100-day project does accomplish is a description that creates a flow of movement toward getting this project out of the mind of the leader and into the physical world, where action can occur. In addition, someone coaching this principal can read his 100-day project plan and begin to understand what he wants to accomplish, and what he thinks is the best way forward.

100-Day Project Strategies

No two 100-day projects are alike. Because every educational system has different cultures and contexts, even if two leaders undertake a 100-day project with the same title and to accomplish the same outcomes, their strategies or approaches for getting the project off the ground are likely to differ. Strategies are the main approaches leaders use to focus the actions they intend to take to implement their project and meet milestones and deadlines (Allison, 2010a: Reeves and Allison, 2009). For example, Exhibit 9.3 compares the strategies selected by two different elementary school principals, both with the same project: "Build teacher networks that use data to improve student achievement."

By looking at the project strategies employed by each of the two principals in Exhibit 9.3, we can make a few inferences about the context surrounding each leader. In the case of principal A, we get the notion that this elementary school requires initial professional development on the work of Data Teams, and structures for leading Data Team meetings and sharing findings. In the case of principal B,

Example Strategies

School Principal A: "Build teacher networks that use data to improve student achievement."	School Principal B: "Build teacher networks that use data to improve student achievement."
Strategy 1: Provide professional development about school-based Data Teams and the five-step Data Teams Process to all teachers.	**Strategy 1:** Revise the schedule to assure three hours of common planning time for teachers of the same courses to meet together.
Strategy 2: Identify grade-level Data Team leaders and provide them with specialized training for efficiently running Data Team meetings.	**Strategy 2:** Select four courses in math and language arts in which teachers will develop and give common assessments on the power standards.
Strategy 3: Hold an "in-house" data fair at the end of the first quarter so that teams can share their strategies and results so far.	**Strategy 3:** Share the results of this work through multiple public methods; for example: prominently displayed data wall, presentation to school board, write-up in parent newsletter, presentations by the teachers at faculty development meetings.

we glean the idea that this school context requires schedule refinements so that teachers have time to meet together to develop common formative assessments and share the results after students take them in select classes of math and language arts.

Principals are responsible for implementing projects with awareness of and concern for the context of the organizational system surrounding them. To not be aware of where projects can begin within the system is to set the project up for failure. Coaches can help leaders set up their projects with effective opening strategies by asking some of the following questions:

- "Where do you see an invitation within the system for this project to start?"
- "What seems to be the natural place for the people in your system to become involved in this project?"
- "What currently exists in the system to support this project?"
- "Where can this project begin to take hold?"
- "Who wants to take part in this project? What do they bring to the table?"
- "Where in the system are the greatest learning needs related to this project?"
- "What would get this project off the ground?"
- "Where are people in the system ready to begin that is part of this project?"

Project strategies are the opening approaches leaders use to get their project moving. As projects progress, the approaches leaders use to keep them moving will change. Leaders should begin with just three opening strategies that match the context and climate of the system they work within. Once the opening strategies are identified, leaders can identify high-impact actions to get the strategies working.

High-Impact Actions

The actions written into the sample plan depicted in Exhibit 9.2 can be sorted into four broad categories: learning, evidence, attitudes, and decisions—otherwise known as L.E.A.D. (Reeves and Allison, 2009 and 2010):

"L"—Learning: Leaders of successful projects assure that they and others build their knowledge and expertise. This category serves as a reminder that the best leaders engage in learning in order to make wise decisions that lead to excellence. Populate your100-day project with actions that require yourself and others to learn. Here are some examples of learning actions:

- Plan and implement professional development experiences geared to the roles and needs of each stakeholder group.

- Engage in book and article studies.

- Hold focus groups and conversations about the ideas in the project.

- Conduct action research projects.

- Explore Web sites and visit other exemplary programs.

- Be mentored by someone who is an expert in the topics of the project.

"E"—Evidence: Leaders must consider relevant information from multiple points of view in order to fully illuminate the issue. Leaders who take time to analyze and discuss relevant evidence create more accurate and complete pictures for themselves and others to see. Populate your 100-day project with actions that require yourself and others to collect, analyze, report, and post data (quantitative and qualitative). What evidence do you have to inform your decisions (data, examples, facts from different points of view)? Here are some examples of evidence actions:

- Determine what student achievement and adult action data to analyze.

- Convene focus groups about the topics in the project and analyze the transcripts for trends and themes.

- Create mini case studies.

- Display data.

- Maintain logs of strategies and their impact.

- Identify the key indicators to identify and monitor.

- Celebrate early wins.

"A"—**Attitude:** Leaders must keep in mind that human beings respond emotionally to projects and the changes they bring. During any change process, emotions play a role. Sometimes individuals and teams are eager to improve but are afraid of how their roles will change. Leaders must remember to look at how their attitudes impact their projects as well. Populate your 100-day project with actions that take into account the emotional side of motivating people to change. Here are some examples of attitude actions:

- Communicate the vision early and often. Be sure to describe how the new initiative benefits all stakeholders.

- Involve individuals and teams in designing their roles and responsibilities in the new reality.

- Keep a journal of the implementation process, noting how you feel about events.

- Set personal learning goals and ask others to do the same.

- Identify the potential challenges and brainstorm ways to mitigate them.

- Establish supportive relationships and networks.

"D"—**Decisions:** Projects require action. At the end of the day, decisions reveal exactly what has changed. Once the learning, evidence, and emotions have been considered, decisions show that the project is moving forward. Populate your 100-day project with actions that create a new result, or represent a choice. Examples of decision actions include:

- Roles and responsibilities
- Policies, guidelines, and practices
- Resources
- Teams
- Schedules
- Deadlines

- Data to monitor

- Information to share and receive

- Structure

Leaders who premeditate actions that are known to move projects forward and reflect on them through coaching conversations put themselves ahead of the curve. The categories of actions presented in the L.E.A.D. framework supply leaders with the tools needed to execute their projects successfully.

Using L.E.A.D. as a Parallel Process during the Coaching Conversation

Coaches can also use L.E.A.D. during the coaching conversation in order to guide them as they develop strong mediating questions to engage their coachees. Questions about learning, evidence, attitude, and decisions cause leaders to *think about* learning, evidence, attitude, and decisions. For example, coaches could say:

1. "Tell me more about what you see as the greatest learning need of each stakeholder group." *(learning)*

2. "How do you envision using the data to guide and reflect on this project?" *(evidence)*

3. "What other people in the school faculties care deeply about making this project a success? How do you envision their roles?" *(attitude)*

4. "How could these decisions leverage resources and systems for future projects?" *(decisions)*

As a parallel tool, the L.E.A.D. framework guides coachees to think deeply about how to make focused headway in their project. Coaches who use the L.E.A.D. framework in their coaching practice feel confident that the questions they ask coachees to encourage reflection will truly be in service to the coachees.

Getting the Most Out of the 100-Day Project

100-day projects are personal working plans for leading projects. They should never be an exercise in compliance. If leaders develop 100-day projects simply to satisfy a requirement for someone else, the plan will become impractical and ineffective. Ideally, leaders who work with a coach use their 100-day project to focus the coaching conversations. Developing the 100-day project should not be an ordeal. What matters is that projects operationalize the mission of the organization. Here are 10 suggestions for leaders who want to develop useful 100-day projects (adapted from Allison, 2010a):

1. Select a project already on your plate that, if accomplished, could make a great difference in your organization. Pick a project that:

   • Directly impacts student achievement.

   • Requires the use of research-based strategies.

   • Calls for leadership and goes beyond your usual "to-do" list.

   • Has a definite implementation date and clear milestones.

   • Builds in regular monitoring of important indicators that show early wins.

2. Identify to yourself why this project matters for all stakeholders. Answer this question and share your thoughts with others: "How will accomplishing this project strengthen the organization?"

3. Tell others about your project and ask them for their support and feedback.

4. Identify in advance when you will measure and report on indicators that show short-term wins.

5. Populate the plan with high-impact actions. Use the L.E.A.D. tool to help you do this:

- Learning: Actions that require you and others to learn.
- Evidence: Actions that require collecting, analyzing, and using data to guide decisions.
- Attitude: Actions that challenge unhelpful attitudes (yours and others') and that support emotions and attitudes that are helpful to the project.
- Decisions: Actions that are decision points.

6. Build in actions that require you to learn and try out helpful leadership behaviors as you roll out your project. Look for ways to overcome your personal leadership Achilles heel.

7. Update your project weekly. Remember, your 100-day project plan allows you to premeditate the most powerful actions needed to move your project forward in the first 100 days. Do not let a week go by without reviewing these actions and revising them as needed.

8. When you feel discouraged, take action from within your circle of control to move your project forward.

9. Reflect with a coach.

10. Teach one other person how to use the 100-day plan to accomplish a project that matters to them.

Leaders use 100-day projects to jump-start initiatives that align with the mission of the organization. 100-day projects, combined with coaching, provide the opportunity for deep reflection about learning as a leader.

PART 4

Coaching
Relationships

CHAPTER TEN

Leaders Who Coach

BIG IDEAS IN CHAPTER TEN

► Good leaders coach.

► Coaches must be comfortable with not having all the answers. They need to embrace perspectives that empower and allow others to uncover their own wisdom.

► Leaders who become known as excellent coaches create a climate around coaching that builds trust. Coaching leaders are trustworthy and confidential in all areas of their work and life.

► Educational leaders cannot possibly know everything that specialists on their teams know. Coaching is a way for leaders to be of service to the people they support, without knowing all the answers.

► Leaders who coach develop discernment about when coaching is and is not the appropriate response to offer colleagues and the people they supervise.

Leading Through Coaching

Great leaders develop other people in the organizations in which they lead. Coaching supports individuals in handling the situations that confront them while simultaneously causing reflection about what it takes to respond well to whatever comes up. This makes coaching a particularly effective approach for developing leaders. Leaders who coach more, lead more (Allison, 2010a), and leaders in education have ample opportunities to coach peers, colleagues, and the people they supervise. In their excellent book, *Execution: The discipline of getting things done* (2002), Bossidy and Charan say, "Coaching is the single most important part of expanding others' capabilities … (Coaching) is the difference between giving orders and teaching people how to get things done. Good leaders regard every encounter as an opportunity to coach" (p. 74). Coaching develops leaders because it provides people with access to their thoughts, and thoughts contain wisdom, even if that wisdom is just an inkling—just a small seed. Coaching activates the potential within the seed (Reeves and Allison, 2009). Fledgling leaders benefit from opportunities to reflect and make decisions in the company of a leader who is devoted to helping them think, rather than providing them with answers that short-change the potential in the moment for growth.

Trust

Leaders who coach within the organization where they work must take extra care to create conditions of safety and trust in which coachees feel that they can, within the confines of coaching, say whatever needs to be said, including hopes, fears, anxieties, and desires, and that they can explore all ideas—even ones that seem risky and reflect on successes and perceived failures. This level of trust demands that leaders who coach do not judge or criticize their coachees or the ideas of their coachees. In addition, coaching leaders must keep their opinions and war stories to themselves, must believe in the coachees and everything they see as possible (and even more than what the coachees see as possible), and must stay true and committed to the agenda the coachees set out to accomplish.

It should go without saying that leaders who coach must have a reputation for being confidential and trustworthy, not just when they are in coaching mode, but in all aspects of their leadership work. Leaders who coach cannot expect to be utilized as coaches if they demonstrate untrustworthiness when they are not wearing the coaching hat. Most people will not and should not give a second chance to a coach who cannot keep confidences. But creating a climate of safety and trust requires more than confidentiality. Leaders who coach must also show up for all agreements to meet for coaching, must not allow interruptions of the coaching sessions, must utilize appropriate coaching tools and strategies, and must follow through on any and all commitments made to the coachee.

Opportunities to Coach

Schools and districts abound with opportunities to coach, every day. In educational systems in which coaching is a widely accepted practice, individuals in all roles can assume the role of coach. For example, we might see principals coaching teachers as they solve challenges of student learning in the classroom. We see principals and other administrators coaching colleagues who seek them out for professional discourse and problem solving. We see teacher leaders coaching team members, and we see specialists coaching principals and teachers alike. At the central office level, we see colleagues coaching each other on curriculum projects and we see cabinet members coaching each other to make great decisions about policies and procedures.

Instilling a culture of coaching within an educational organization often begins with the first offer of "coaching" from one person to another. Consider the following conversation between a principal and a lead teacher.

Carrie is a lead teacher in a Pre-K–5 elementary school in Wisconsin. She is an effective teacher; her students learn and they love coming to school. Carrie is also a teacher leader in the school and in the district. For the last two years, she has served as team leader for the fifth grade. In this role, Carrie facilitates the Professional Learning Community meetings (Dufour and Eaker, 1998) of the fifth-grade teachers. In the first year of leading the fifth-grade team, Carrie implemented a process for the teachers to score student work together and track the percentage of students becoming proficient in critical standards each month. The team even agreed to put a growth chart up in the hallway so that the fifth-grade students and their teachers could see at a glance the growth of the entire grade level. In the first few months of putting up the visual displays of growth data, Carrie and her team noticed positive changes in student learning. They were all very excited. It was as if just the simple act of tracking data had an impact on student achievement.

But after a few months, the data began to level out. Carrie knew from her team leader training that the teachers needed to move on from just tracking data with current classroom approaches, to using the data to identify powerful classroom strategies and interventions to help more students learn at higher levels. Moreover, once they identified the strategies, the teachers needed to actually follow through and apply the strategies with focus and deliberation in their classrooms. They also needed to meet regularly to discover how the strategies they agreed to use work with different groups of students, and they needed to adjust and revise their use of the strategies to keep them vibrant and effective.

When Carrie shared her observations about this process with the fifth-grade team, she met with some resistance that took the form of complaints about the time these additional meetings would take. One influential teacher on the team told Carrie, "Look, what we are doing is already working. The student data show gains—maybe not as fast as we want (or for all students, Carrie thought to herself...), but gains all the same. We just have to keep going, doing what we each do best in our classrooms. We don't need to meet more often or use the same strategies to be effective."

Carrie felt discouraged by her team's reaction. She began to doubt her ability to serve as team leader. She decided she needed to meet with her principal, Dr. Jones, to ask what she should do to get her team in gear. In the back of her mind, she also thought that maybe it was time to step down as team leader.

What if Principal Jones coached Carrie about this dilemma instead of providing her with answers? What would become possible for each fifth-grade teacher, for the team, and for Carrie as a teacher leader? Let's imagine how Principal Jones might begin a coaching conversation with Carrie:

> CARRIE: "Principal Jones, do you have a minute? I'd like to tell you about a problem I'm having on my grade-level team. I just can't get them to follow through and implement the classroom strategies that we agreed to use with our students."

> PRINCIPAL JONES: "Carrie, now is a great time—I'd be happy to coach you on that."

> CARRIE: "What do you mean, 'coach me'?"

> PRINCIPAL JONES: "I'll listen to you as you tell me about the situation you are facing with your team, and then I will ask you some questions that will help you think out loud about the details and nuances. I won't give you advice or tell you what you need to do, but I'm certain you'll leave here in 20 minutes with some great ideas you can begin tomorrow. You see, coaching is a process that inspires insight and action."

> CARRIE: "That sounds good. You're right. What I really want is to understand what I can do to help the team break through this current barrier. It seems so impossible now, but I know other teams are doing it, so we can too."

In this case study, Principal Jones did not have to provide long explanations about what coaching entails. She just needed to recognize that the situation presented by Carrie, and Carrie's desire to grow as a leader, was a great opportunity for coaching.

Empowering Others

As presented in Chapter Two, leaders wear many different hats during the course of any given day. Sometimes leaders supervise, sometimes they mentor, sometimes they teach and collaborate, and sometimes they consult and advise. When coaching is the most effective way to support others, the outcomes are extremely positive for the coachee, and they create forward movement in the organization. As simple as it might look to begin a coaching conversation, as we saw with Principal Jones and Teacher Leader Carrie, leaders who coach work hard at staying in the coaching role.

Coaching is more about developing other people than dispensing advice and making recommendations. In fact, many experienced and effective leaders come to the stunning realization that until they quit having all the answers, they were not really leading at all (Hargrove, 2007). Hence, coaching demands a disciplined ego. Some leaders who choose to coach their peers, colleagues, and the people they supervise find it challenging to restrain the desire or need to "be the one with all the answers." More than other professionals, educators tend to find this coaching requirement quite challenging, presumably because they work in systems in which, from the classroom to the board room, having answers and getting things right is highly valued and always rewarded. Once a leader agrees to coach a peer, colleague, or someone they supervise, however, they must *coach*. They must resist falling back into the more comfortable roles of mentoring, consulting, and supervising. Even in blended models of coaching, where coaches might instruct a novice principal, for example, in a certain method or process combined with facilitating the principal's reflection about what they learned (Bloom, et al., 2005), being clear about which modes of support are in play at any given moment reduces ambiguity, confusion, and mischief (Allison, 2010a).

When to Coach

Leaders who embrace coaching as a way of supporting others notice opportunities to coach during the workday and choose to do so as often as possible. Even though coaching might initially take more time to conduct than, let's say, just giving an opinion would take, these leaders recognize that coaching may, in fact, be the best job-embedded professional development approach available, especially after teachers have learned new ideas and now want to apply them in their work and practice. In their now famous 1995 study about the impact of coaching on teachers implementing new skills to create change in teaching and learning, Bruce Joyce and Beverley Showers have shown that without coaching, only 5 to 15 percent of what teachers learn in other models of professional development (presentation, modeling, practice, and low-risk feedback in a workshop) make it to the classroom.

Coaching is not a panacea. It cannot possibly replace other forms of supporting people, such as mentoring, teaching, collaborating, or supervising when they are undeniably more appropriate to the coachee and to the situation. Leaders who coach develop a knack for recognizing when coaching is the best leadership approach to offer.

Here are some conditions that make coaching a powerful way to impact others (adapted from Allison, 2010a):

1. **When coachees have projects in mind and feel excited about seeing them implemented.** Coachees who express passion for carrying out a project they are responsible for are rewarding to coach. If these coachees know and understand the value of coaching, they may seek out a colleague who can coach them as they carry out their project strategies and respond thoughtfully to the challenges that come up. Leaders who coach are fortunate when someone with a passionate project asks to be coached. Coachees who invite leaders to coach them are more likely to participate fully in each coaching conversation and take action to cre-

ate change after each conversation. Leaders who coach also seek out and offer their time as coaches to those who have a passionate project but may not know that they can ask for coaching.

2. **When coachees come to the leader with a specific situation or dilemma and they also have ideas for proactively addressing it**. Sometimes on-the-job coaching is more situational than project-based. Even so, to qualify as coaching, it must lead to action taken by coachees. In school systems, leaders at all levels run into situations that are barriers to them as they work with others and carry out their responsibilities. A good example of this is Carrie, the fifth-grade teacher leader who needed to reflect on and plan for ways to move her team forward in an area in which they were resisting progress. Even though she was feeling a certain degree of powerlessness, Carrie approached Principal Jones with ideas. She knew the team needed to begin looking at student work and implementing agreed-upon strategies. With coaching from Principal Jones, Carrie can more fully explore the ideas she has and create avenues that inspire action and movement forward.

3. **When development of coachees is just as important as or more important than completing the projects or tasks.** Leaders know that one of their primary responsibilities is to develop other leaders. Moreover, they seek ways to provide leadership development opportunities on the job, where the context provides "real-time" situations that demand attention, decisions, and action. What could be more perfect than to have the opportunity to coach someone who is going about accomplishing the mission of the school or district? Yet, task completion is usually time-bound and the coaching process takes more time than it takes to simply tell someone what they should do. Leaders

who coach more often choose to take more time and allow the task to be a day late rather than compromise a perfect opportunity to facilitate meaningful on-the-job development with a person who shows great promise as a leader. Sure, coaching may take longer, and important tasks might be delayed a day or two. But the gains that come from coaching bring compounded returns. Not only are tasks accomplished, but they are often accomplished better than they would have been without coaching, *and* the coachee's capacity for accomplishing this task and similar tasks in the future increases.

4. **When coachees are dependent on answers and advice from others and lack confidence in their ability to know what to do and take action.** As we go about our lives, the world operates on us and we operate on the world. For good or ill, people and their surrounding environments undergo both profound and subtle changes. While it would be great if all human beings felt capable and prepared to respond to everything that comes up at all times, some life experiences take the wind out of our sails and erode our confidence. Some adults become so afraid of making a mistake that they simply won't make a move unless they consult the person they see as being in charge or the person who will criticize them, or worse, if they fail (Mezirow, 2000). Leaders who coach seek to elevate the capabilities of those around them by empowering them with pathways to discover their own answers to the dilemmas they face. As with most outcomes of coaching, both leaders who coach and their coachees enjoy reciprocal benefits (Reeves and Allison, 2009). Leaders who coach the people around them eventually gain more time and energy to lead, and their coachees gain more ownership of and accountability for their actions.

5. **When coachees ultimately need to take responsibility for how their projects turn out or how situations are addressed and resolved.** Leaders who coach and who become known for coaching within their organization are sought after by peers and colleagues who need to accomplish projects that could make or break a career, a program, or even the mission of the school and district. Although leaders rarely carry out high-stakes projects alone, they are often at the helm of highly visible projects in the district or organization and they will receive both the accolades for things that go right and the criticism for things that go wrong, with the latter making for more interesting news fodder than the former. Coaching does not guarantee that high-stakes projects will run perfectly or turn out exactly as visualized. But coaching does build in important time for reflection that most leaders rarely have as they make crucial decisions, work with others, and carry out important work. At the very least, leaders who have a coach as they implement high-stakes projects have a deeper understanding of the reasoning and data behind each of their decisions. This gives coachees greater confidence as they convey information to others or are asked to justify the decisions they made.

When Not to Coach

Leaders who coach must also develop a level of discernment that guides them to know when coaching is not the best model for supporting a colleague or someone they supervise. Some situations in which coaching is not the appropriate response are obvious. These include emergencies, or when an immediate answer is required and time is of the essence. Other situations are more nuanced and require a contextual decision. Some leaders cannot honestly coach when they feel a conflict of interest, such as when they have strong opinions about the coachee's project or plan and what should be done, or they feel there is only one "right" answer, or when they simply dislike the other person. In addition, unless they are using a coaching model specific to performance improvement, leaders should not coach someone who is struggling. Other situations when coaching may or may not be the right response include situations where coachees are new to the requirements of the project and they do not have transferable skills, or when the potential coachee refuses to be coached.

Leaders who coach for the educational system they work within provide their colleagues and direct reports with one of the best job-embedded professional development models known. The benefits to the leader, the people they lead and coach, and the organization compound and have a ripple effect.

In Chapter Eleven, we will explore ideas about the portals to coaching that open up during the workday and give leaders who coach opportunities to support and develop others every day.

CHAPTER ELEVEN

Pulling the Coaching Relationship Together

BIG IDEAS IN CHAPTER ELEVEN

► Leaders who want coaching over a period of time enter into a coaching agreement with their coach.

► Coaching is an agreement between two people, one who wants to accomplish an important project and grow as a leader and another who wants to support leaders.

► Coaching agreements are explicit and both parties have obligations to the other.

► Coaches keep notes to create historical records of their coachee's project so they can make systemic and relevant connections to aid the coachee.

► Organizations that implement a consistent coaching approach can evaluate the impact of coaching on student achievement, leadership development, and organizational change.

Let the Coaching Begin

Coaching relationships most often begin with leaders requesting coaching from other leaders they know, either within the system or outside the system, who are also known for being great coaches. We have already established the requirement that great coaches support leaders in accomplishing important work that makes a difference in the organization and that might not otherwise be done as well if the leader had not sought the support of a coach. Good coaches enter every single coaching agreement with a commitment to the leaders who ask for their support.

Have the "Agreement Conversation"

The first coaching conversation ever is different from the coaching conversations to follow. Before coaching can begin, understanding must be achieved and agreements must be established about the nature of the coachee's project as well as the desired outcomes of coaching. The first conversation usually lasts between one and two hours and is designed to achieve the following tasks:

1. Introductions and conversation about the coachee's experience with coaching, how the coachee feels about coaching, and what the coachee hopes to gain from coaching.

2. Descriptions of the coachee's project, including the desired vision and outcomes. This part of the agreement conversation also establishes the current state of the coachee's project in *juxtaposition* to the desired vision. This is sometimes called a "gap analysis." The gap analysis makes visible the difference between the vision of the project and the current state of the project. The gap analysis begins to make apparent the actions the coachee wants to take to literally close the gap until the vision is realized (Kilburg, 2000). This conversation leads to the creation of the 100-day project as outlined in Chapter Nine of this book. Coachees often find it helpful to create the 100-day project plan right then and there, during the first conversation, with the assistance of the coach. Once the 100-day

project plan is created, coaches and coachees refer to it in each coaching conversation, especially at the start of the session, when the coachee reflects on how the actions they took after the last conversation turned out, and at the end of the session, when the coachee is planning next steps.

3. Answer any questions and address any worries the coachee has about the coaching process, agreements, confidentiality, roles, responsibilities, and mutual expectations. Remember that most leaders rarely have the opportunity to think through what matters to them without other people jumping in, giving advice, and telling stories about their own experiences. As a result, they might find coaching uncomfortable at first, especially if the coach is mindful about not making the coaching session about how much the coach knows.

4. Review the coaching agreement (see a sample coaching agreement template in Appendix B), clarify the ideas in

EXHIBIT 11.1 **Sample Agenda for the Agreement Conversation**

- Introductions.

- A discussion about who or what brought you together as coach and coachee.

- An overview of the coaching process and details about how the conversation works.

- Decisions about logistical procedures such as dates, meeting place, the use of telephone and other technology.

- A discussion of confidentiality and the coaching agreement.

- Identification of the coaching project and development of the plan for the first 100 days.

the agreement as needed, and answer questions. Both the coach and the coachee should sign the agreement at the end of the conversation.

5. After the agreement conversation, the coach should send a brief e-mail recapping the conversation, confirming the name of the project, and listing the dates of the rest of the scheduled coaching conversations (if the coach and coachee do not schedule the full complement of meetings during the first conversation, this e-mail should include, at a minimum, the next three scheduled meetings). The e-mail should also include any other important information that may have come up during the conversation.

Scheduling the Coaching Conversations

Coaches and coachees who are serious about accomplishing important work, and who agree to work together over an extended period of time (as opposed to having a single impromptu coaching conversation), schedule the series of coaching conversations in advance for the entire time they agree to work with each other. Together, coaches and coaches place these conversations on their calendars and they make certain that the coaching sessions appear on any calendars shared by administrative assistants. This secures the time for coaching and firmly conveys the value that coaching matters in the organization.

Often, coaches who are external to the leader's system dedicate certain days and times each week for coaching. External coaches who coach only on certain days each week or month need to determine how flexible they can be and want to be to accommodate a coachee who is not available on the days and times they have set aside for coaching. Most external coaches do everything they can to work with their coachees' schedules. However, leaders should be aware that most external coaches do not reschedule coaching sessions missed by coachees or canceled with less than one day of notice. Leaders who coach and are internal to the system also have full-time responsibilities within their own leadership position. These leaders often limit their long-term coaching agreements to one or two peers, colleagues, or direct reports at a time. However, just like coaches who are external to the system, leaders who coach must schedule these coaching conversations and diligently keep each and every commitment to meet with the people they have agreed to coach.

Organize Information

Long-term coaching agreements require a certain amount of organizing structures that allow both the coach and the coachee to benefit from a fluid and dependable coaching experience. Long-term coaching agreements mean that this coach and coachee plan to stay together in this unique relationship until a project is safely launched or even completed. Many coachees have the same coach for years. The longer the coaching relationship, the more important it is that the coach have a system for organizing and accessing important information shared by the coachee, for the history of the project or projects.

With experience, reflective coaches develop organizing systems that match their personal strengths. Here are some practical tips:

- Create an electronic folder for your coaching work with a separate folder inside for each coachee. Keep all documents for the client inside that folder (coaching agreement, 100-day project plan, notes, calendar of coaching schedule, copies of e-mails, and coaching journal for each coachee).

- Create a coaching journal (see a sample coaching journal template in Appendix C) for each coachee. This is where you can take notes about each conversation. These notes are confidential. They are often rough notes that contain not only what the coachee said but sometimes also contain your reflections as you focus on what matters to the coachee.

• Keep a master calendar of the coaching conversations you have with all coachees so you can easily add them up when you need to. This is especially important if the coachee or another person in the system the coachee works within has asked you, as part of the coaching agreement, to provide feedback on the number of coaching conversations you've provided for a certain person or persons.

Coaching Notes and Journal

Leaders who coach their peers and colleagues on their most important projects have an obligation and commitment to create a historical record of the progression of the projects and goals. Personally, while in the coaching conversation I simply write down most of what my coachees say; not word for word, but I do keep my notes running as coachees speak. As I write, what I call my "coach's mind" is actively engaged in discerning what seems to be most important to my coachees and to my coachee's project, goals, and the focus of the conversation.

The point is, all coaches need to establish a journal that contains an organized framework for capturing important information for each of their coachees. I advise novice coaches to set up a two-sided journal. On the right-hand side, coaches write notes about what coachees say during each coaching session. Important elements to record include an **update** of the project and how the actions the coachee committed to at the end of the previous conversation turned out when they were actually carried out. Other elements to include on the right-hand side are the **focus** of the conversation, **notes** from the conversation, and finally, the **commitments** the coachee made at the end of the conversation.

On the left-hand side, the journal provides a space for coaches to track their own thoughts about the coaching process. For example, on the left-hand side, coaches might write observations about where they think clarification about certain aspects of the project

EXHIBIT 11.2 **Example Two-Sided Journal**

My Reflections/Questions about the Coaching Conversation	Notes from the Coaching Conversation
I found a way to ask questions when I want to be sure that Jack has covered certain details. Instead of asking what is what about something, I added this preamble: "Jack, if this is something you've already got covered, tell me and we can move on to the next thought instead of you feeling like you have to explain it to me." I really like how this preamble helped us stay on track. Jack did not feel obligated to give me the entire rationale for decisions already made. Instead, we had more time to actually discuss the actions he wanted to take to move his project forward.	**Date: September 14, 2007** **UPDATE:** Jack did not have a chance to observe the teams in action because he discovered a fluke in the schedule. **FOCUS:** Put together a schedule for meeting with teachers one-on-one about their classroom student achievement data. Wants the data meetings to be rigorous but welcoming, so teachers do not become defensive. **NOTES:** Assistant Principal put a schedule together but overlooked some inconsistencies, which left a few teachers with planning times other than when their team was meeting. Work from the priority academic standards. Teachers are empowered when they present the data. Could ask them to do a presentation to highlight strengths and challenges. This makes talking about difficulties part of the process instead of a "gotcha." **COMMITMENTS:** Jack agreed to these actions to move his project forward: • Write out the specs for the schedule for the Assistant Principal to use as a checklist as the schedule is developed. • Get a small group of teachers to help put together (in one hour) the agenda and protocol for the data meetings.

will help their coachees. Or, they might write words their coachees say that convey strong emotions that might be helpful to return to during the current conversation or subsequent conversations. Exhibit 11.2 shows a condensed example of a two-sided journal.

After coaches write or type their journal notes, they copy and paste summary information into an e-mail that they send to their coachees when each conversation ends. Most important to include in this follow-up e-mail are the commitments of the coachee to move their project forward, anything that the coach promised (such as to send an article or share a protocol or a book or reference information), and the date of the next coaching conversation. I also advise coaches to copy themselves on the e-mail memo and then save it to the file of the coachee. In Appendix C, there is a coaching journal set up for two coaching conversations per month. Please adapt this journal to fit your particular situation.

Monitoring Coaching Agreements and Ongoing Accountability for Coach and Coachee

Progress monitoring of the coaching agreement achieves three important outcomes. First, it shows that the coach cares about the coachee and the project of the coachee. Second, it builds in opportunities to adjust the coaching process so that it works well for each coachee. Third, it builds in mutual accountability between the coach and coachee. Coaches have strategies for monitoring the progress of the coaching agreement and assuring that both parties follow through on the commitments made. Leaders who coach peers and colleagues under a long-term agreement see progress monitoring as an important part of the coaching strategy.

To monitor progress, show concern, and assure accountability in long-term coaching agreements, coaches need to:

1. Have a minimum of three dates, or preferably, all coaching dates and times, on the calendar at any given time.

Coaches should send an e-mail reminder to coachees the day before each coaching conversation.

2. Ask at the beginning of each conversation: "What will we have accomplished at the end of this conversation that will be a success?" Ask at the end of each conversation: "Did we accomplish what you hoped we would, now that our conversation is concluded?"

The accountability measure: The percentage of occasions when the answer to the second question is "Yes." This can be tracked for each client as well as for your caseload overall.

3. End each coaching conversation with a list of commitment actions the coachee will take between now and the next coaching session. The next session begins with a reference to the commitments made at the end of the previous session.

• "How did the new schedule turn out? Tell me about that."

• "How did you feel about your conversation with the superintendent?"

4. For each commitment, ask coachees what might come up to prevent them from accomplishing what they committed to do. This shows that you want them to stay on track and encourages them to imagine ways to confront barriers to success.

5. Write important notes about the conversation in the journal during the coaching conversation or as soon as possible after the coaching conversation. Save it to the file established for each coachee and e-mail the summary and commitments to the coachee.

6. Coaches should ask their coachees to send them a quick memo or text message when they accomplish something on the list of commitment actions. For example:

"Hi Elle—just wanted you to know the scheduled meeting went great today! Will tell you about it during our call on Thursday."

The Final Conversation

The final coaching conversation between coaches and their coachees provides a time for celebration, reflection, and feedback. Although coaches seek formative feedback at the end of each individual coaching conversation, they seek summative feedback about the effectiveness of coaching during the final conversation of the long-term agreement.

Here are some accountability ideas that coaches should bear in mind as they seek feedback in the last coaching conversation:

1. **Listen for efficacy in coachees.** Coachees should never feel dependent on their coach. This does not mean that the goal of coaching is to eliminate the desire for coaching. In fact, many highly effective leaders are those who have never been without a coach. Coaching gives leaders a performance edge, so why would a leader not want to have a coach? The point is that coachees should see the coaching as valuable for what it allows them to accomplish, not for what a coach tells them to do. If coaches hear feedback from coachees that refers to their sage advice, or personal experiences shared, they need to take a good look at how they present themselves when coaching. Great coaches prefer feedback about the quality of the questions they asked that facilitated insights within their coachees over accolades for providing ideas and advice.

2. **Listen for what coachees say they have accomplished.** Leaders seek coaching when they want to accomplish remarkable outcomes aligned with the mission of the organization. The outcomes your coachee identified at the

start of the process, as well as at the start of each conversation, are useful indicators. These data can be collected and reported to a third party without revealing the content of the coaching conversation. Questions coaches ask include: Did you complete the milestones so far in your project? Does your project advance the goals of the organization? What feedback have you received from your coworkers about the impact your project has had on the organization? Coachees can also choose to survey people on their team or in the organization regarding changes they saw or did not see. If the leader wishes to have this sort of feedback, which is also a reflection of your coaching, it needs to be agreed to up front.

Evaluating the Impact of Leadership Performance Coaching on Your Organization

Beyond the accountability that coaches and their coachees have to each other to accomplish projects that improve the organization, leaders might also evaluate the long-term impact of a consistent coaching approach. In order to understand the impact coaching has had in your educational organization, relative to leadership development, student achievement, and contribution to the development of the organization, leaders should consider the following elements:

• Establish and implement a consistent coaching program in your organization and commit to it for at least three years, which will allow you to analyze trend data. For example, provide coaching for the same leaders in the same role for three years, where the coach and the coachee engage in at least two coaching conversations per month, for a minimum of six months per year, focused on accomplishing an important project that is critical to the goals of the organization.

- Establish baseline student achievement data from the year *before* the consistent coaching practice began, in the schools where the leader's coaching project is meant to have an impact. For example, if the coachee is a principal, then look at student achievement data in his or her school. If the coachee is a central office employee, let's say with a coaching project to revise a particular subject area curriculum or instructional practices in a specific subject area or grade level, establish the baseline the year before the coaching began by aggregating data from all the sites where the coaching project will have an impact.

- From the baseline points, collect, chart, display, and discuss the same results for three years.

- Seek information from the coachees about what things the coaches did that were helpful (Vanderburg and Stephens, 2010) and how they view the impact of the coaching project on the organization. For example, ask leaders who have been coached to rate the extent to which they took action in their project to achieve specific milestones and the relationship between their project and important changes in the organization.

- Consider asking the leaders who have been coached to rate their growth as leaders. You can also ask other people in the leader's school building, department, or, for top leaders (superintendents and others), district or organization to rate the same characteristics.

Coaching is an organizational strategy for making important and valued changes for people and for the system. As such, it should be evaluated for effectiveness and impact in the same spirit that other important initiatives and strategies in the organization are evaluated. You don't have to go overboard on this; focus on looking at student achievement over time, and specific information about what coaches did that made a difference for the leaders they coached.

This approach to evaluating your leadership coaching strategy will provide you with the ability to make good decisions about how to improve your coaching program and where to scale it up (if it is indeed successful) within the organization.

PART 5

Becoming
a Great
Coach

Called to Coaching

BIG IDEAS IN CHAPTER TWELVE

► Although the profession of coaching is not regulated, poor coaches are weeded out by savvy coachees.

► Coaches gain credibility by supporting coachees to accomplish important work and gain leadership abilities.

► Ineffective coaches deplete leaders and organizations.

► Effective coaches have a clear mission for their work and a framework that guides the coaching process.

► Effective coaches engage in ongoing and lifelong learning.

Some educators picked up this book because they feel drawn to doing the work of a coach. Whether you are an educator who coaches your peers, colleagues, and direct reports within your school or district, or you are a coach who works external to the organization of the leaders you coach, coaching is important and rewarding work.

Coaching Credibility

Great coaching is not easy. Coaches must be accomplished at communication, project management, and coaching processes. They must also devote time and energy to treating every coaching relationship with the professionalism and consideration that it deserves (Ulrich, 2006). Yet, with all of these requirements, coaching is an unregulated field. As such, just about anyone who thinks "coaching is easy" can call themselves a coach and give people the impression that they are qualified to coach. Fortunately, savvy coachees will weed out the poor educational coaches by giving them unfavorable reviews and pointing out their ineffectiveness. The sad thing is, naive coachees might not recognize poor coaching, especially if the coach comes from a credible organization but never took the time to really learn or practice how to be a great coach. In cases like this, coachees may not know that the coach is lacking knowledge, skill and experience, no matter what organization backs them. Individuals who have the title "coach" but lack the disposition, knowledge, skills, and experience of a true coach can do a lot of damage. Here are examples of how ineffective coaches deplete leaders and organizations:

- They do not require coachees to identify a coaching project. Without a coaching project, coaching becomes a series of unrelated conversations that produce very little or nothing to show, to benefit the organization. Educational leaders need to run from coaches who do not understand how to help them set up a coaching project or who find it tedious because *they* have never thoughtfully and rigorously completed a project successfully.

- They are not reflective about each coaching session and therefore are unable to help coachees notice leadership opportunities. Without reflection, coaches cannot help their coachees see where they have grown and where they still need to grow.

- They cannot resist being a "sage on the stage," and so they use coaching sessions to showcase just how clever and experienced they are. They waste precious coaching time delivering minilectures to their coachees who, if they don't know better, come to believe that coaching is an hour chat during which coaches get to show how wise they are. While stories and advice from coaches are interesting at times, coachees cannot use lessons from the past stories of their coach to take action in their current context, and they rarely (thankfully in this case) follow such advice.

- They cannot "get over themselves" and so they use coaching as a way to stay in their past, neglecting the requirement that coaching is in service of the coachee's current context, not the glory days of the coach. Poor coaches often delude themselves into believing that their coachee's situation is just like a situation the coach experienced "back in the day."

- They engage in gossip and/or rumor-mongering, and violate confidentiality, thereby eroding trust between themselves and their coachees. This behavior taints the entire organization and even makes the sponsors of the coaching initiative suspect of looking for ways to catch employees doing the wrong thing.

By default, coachees help regulate the field by refusing to work with coaches who exhibit practices that waste their time and thereby actually diminish their effectiveness as leaders doing important work. Great coaches treat their work with care and respect, seeking always to serve their coachees.

Ask Much of Yourself First

Coaches who make a difference for others are mindful of how they go about their coaching work. Here are some questions aspiring coaches in education must ask themselves:

- How do you want to be known as a coach? Coaches who have a coaching method that supports leaders in accomplishing important work become known as *coaches* who support leaders in accomplishing important work. What do you want to be known for as a coach? What will your reputation be?

• What is your mission as a coach? Coaches make other people shine. They do not and should not get the credit for the good work leaders do. As such, coaching helps individuals reach their full potential (Tracy, 2006). If your personal mission as a coach is to serve others so they can be successful, you are on the right track.

• What is your method and process for coaching? Successful coaches have a framework that clearly defines the coaching process as well as the underlying philosophies. For example, educational coachees who choose to be coached by an employee of The Leadership and Learning Center will experience a method and process that (a) requires a project, (b) focuses on leadership actions to accomplish the project, and (c) closes the gap between the vision of a fully implemented project and the current status. Additionally, these coaches possess a strong knowledge base about the requirements of leadership in education.

Effective coaches, whether they are leaders who coach their peers and colleagues or coaches who are external to the system they provide coaching for, treat the opportunity to coach with reverence. Effective coaches understand that they can make a difference for good or ill in the lives of the leaders they coach and they seek out information and support to become better coaches.

Qualifications of Educational Coaches

Educational leaders who want to work with a coach expect that the coach is knowledgeable about the field of education. They have basic expectations that educational coaches understand the complexity of most school district systems as well as the political climate surrounding national and local educational policies and practices. In addition, they expect their coaches to be up on the lingo and acronyms in education and have knowledge of and even experience with the latest initiatives, research ideas, and topics in education.

Although many educational leaders at the superintendent level expect to work with a coach who has had experience as a superintendent, the truth is that the work of great coaches does not depend at all on the coach having been in the exact same job roles as the people they coach (Reeves and Allison, 2009). More important than role, the educational coach needs to possess a reputation for being or having been an excellent leader, no matter what position they held previously. No one wants to work with coaches who were fired from their previous jobs in education or who have records of poor performance. Many regional and state agencies create coaching programs that employ retired educators as coaches. Provided these coaches stay on top of the best information in the field, and provided they have received excellent training in the skills of coaching, these retired individuals can serve as excellent coaches.

Are You Cut Out to Coach?

If you are drawn to coaching, you will do well to be crystal clear about what the best coaches require of themselves. The following inventory comes from my work with Renewal Coaching (Allison, 2010a). It asks aspiring coaches to honestly assess their comfort level with the philosophical demands of coaching. Consider the questions provided on the survey below and rate yourself according to the levels provided.

1. **Although I am a leader or am known for my expertise, I do not feel obligated to have all the answers.**

This is not me at all						This sounds exactly like me			
1	2	3	4	5	6	7	8	9	10

2. I do not try to have all the answers in order to "look good" to the people around me.

This is not me at all							This sounds exactly like me		
1	2	3	4	5	6	7	8	9	10

3. I am not known as a gossip, nor do I traffic with gossips or offer information about other people in order to be accepted by a group of gossips.

This is not me at all							This sounds exactly like me		
1	2	3	4	5	6	7	8	9	10

4. Even though it would be quicker to solve problems for others, I most often resist doing this and instead help others solve the problems themselves.

This is not me at all							This sounds exactly like me		
1	2	3	4	5	6	7	8	9	10

5. I often know what I think is the right or best answer, but I prefer to bring out expertise in others.

This is not me at all							This sounds exactly like me		
1	2	3	4	5	6	7	8	9	10

6. Leaders exist at all levels in the system and I believe these individuals have unique wisdom and answers.

This is not me at all							This sounds exactly like me		
1	2	3	4	5	6	7	8	9	10

7. The people I lead (or have led in the past) come up with revisions, refinements, and innovative ideas to further the vision of the organization. I trust the wisdom in others that leads them to these visions.

This is not me at all							This sounds exactly like me		
1	2	3	4	5	6	7	8	9	10

8. I have people in my life who listen to me and I have experienced first-hand the value of having time to hear my own thoughts.

This is not me at all						This sounds exactly like me			
1	2	3	4	5	6	7	8	9	10

9. I have tackled difficult projects in my own life and work and have successfully taken action to bring about change or create something meaningful.

This is not me at all						This sounds exactly like me			
1	2	3	4	5	6	7	8	9	10

10. I do not have a need to "save" other people from the discomfort of their struggles and experiences.

This is not me at all						This sounds exactly like me			
1	2	3	4	5	6	7	8	9	10

Reflecting on Your Survey Results

If you have been honest about your ratings, you probably wrestled with at least one of the ideas presented in the survey. This does not mean that you cannot learn to be a great coach. What it does mean is that you need to raise your awareness about these ideas and notice how they influence the way you interact with others and engage with your own work. A good way to do this is to write down any statement for which you scored eight or lower on a sticky note, and keep it with you for a day or more. Read it a few times during the day as you go about your work and notice what it takes for you to move higher on the scale.

Additionally, if you have yet to work with a coach to accomplish an important project on your plate, now would be a good time to engage the services of one. Working with a great coach will require you to experience first-hand what it is to be a coachee (Tracy, 2006). Once you have asked yourself to toe the line with the same requirements you intend to ask of your coachees, you will acquire a sincere level of compassion and authenticity that cannot be learned by reading a book. The Leadership and Learning Center has a team of coaches trained in the Leadership Performance Coaching approach who would be happy to coach you.

There is a vast difference in the competencies, qualities, and effectiveness of coaches between the first person they coach and the 25th person they coach (Axtell, 2009). Serious coaches who are effective in their work with the leaders they coach not only seek as much coaching experience as possible, but they continue to engage in their own professional development as a coach. Leaders who want to work with a coach should refuse to have coaches thrust upon them who do not:

- work with their own coach.
- have training from a qualified program where the instructors are masterful coaches themselves.
- demonstrate that they have developed and worked through their own 100-day project plans.
- deepen their knowledge and practice in coaching by participating in professional development.

Those who work with designing coaching training programs agree that certain activities are essential to the ongoing support and development of coaches (Allison, 2010a; Bloom, et al., 2005; Chen, 2003; Haneberg, 2006). These activities suggest that coaches should:

1. Participate in specific and ongoing learning within quality coach training programs that include practical experience in coaching with feedback.

2. Belong to a professional learning community and network for coaches in order to learn new coaching skills, methods, and techniques.

3. Work with a coach in order to accomplish projects in their own life.

4. Stay current in the research and best ideas of the field in which they coach, including the standards, current practices, interventions, opportunities, and approaches.

5. Acquire specific training in setting up and monitoring projects and become skilled in using the tools that structure project implementation.

6. Immerse themselves in learning events and conversations with others about organizational change processes and human development theory.

Quality coaches who treasure the opportunity to support others through the coaching perspective create personal professional development plans to deepen their knowledge, skill, and practice as coaches. Of course, the most powerful way to evaluate your effectiveness as a coach is to notice and celebrate the wins of the leaders you coach, exactly in the same way an excellent teacher evaluates their impact on students by celebrating each step they make in the direction of their goals and dreams for themselves. Like great teachers, great coaches support their coachees in going even further than they first imagined or even knew was possible.

Called to Coaching

Many people describe coaching as a calling. When asked, both novice and veteran coaches often talk about wanting to help other people and make a difference. They describe feeling joy in watching others accomplish what previously seemed either unattainable or confusing and difficult. They like to see realized potential and they recognize that in the role of coach, they provide the difference that makes all the difference. In addition to these emotional and altruistic motivations, leaders embrace a coaching approach because they identify themselves in the required skill set. They have good communication skills, they listen well, they ask compelling questions, they understand project management, and they are not squeamish when it comes to holding coachees accountable.

In my work as a trainer of coaches, I watch for the "coaching light" to flash in the eyes of the learners in the room. The sparkle gradually brightens as the coach-in-training experiences a few rounds of coaching in the labs that take place in my seminars. Inevitably, a couple of people approach me to say that coaching has been the missing element in their work and career. These leaders get it. They understand that coaching will allow them to develop leaders and accomplish the most important work of the organization.

Coaches who support leaders as they accomplish great things in their schools and districts know just how awe-inspiring coaching can be. The coach's role is to challenge coachees to want more and to take action to fulfill their dearest objectives. It is not an easy journey, but when it works, it is magic.

To learn more about Leadership Performance Coaching, visit The Leadership and Learning Center online at www.leadandlearn.com.

Frequently Asked Questions
from Coaching Clients of
The Leadership and Learning Center

Q: What exactly is Leadership Performance Coaching?

A: Leadership Performance Coaching is a confidential development process for helping you produce the results you want to increase student achievement through a significant leadership project. The coaching process provides a dedicated time for you to think out loud, take action, and be accountable.

Q: Will my coach give me advice and tell me what to do?

A: No. Giving advice is more in line with the role of a consultant. Your coach will skillfully use a conversation process that allows you to think aloud, discover solutions, and commit to actions so you can accomplish the project you define in your 100-day project plan.

Q: When will I hear from my coach? How will my coaching get started?

A: Your Leadership Performance Coach will contact you via e-mail and/or phone to schedule your first coaching conversation. Unless special arrangements have been established, your first conversation will occur sometime within the first two weeks after you ask to be coached.

Q: What are the desired outcomes of the first conversation?

A: (1) Get to know each other and make a commitment to the coaching relationship. (2) Understand Leadership Performance

Coaching and have your questions/concerns addressed. (3) Be clear about the logistics of the coaching sessions: dates, time, methods, updated contact information. (4) Clarify your 100-day leadership project. (5) Confirm the dates of your coaching sessions. (6) Review and sign the coaching agreement. (7) Discuss current student achievement in reading, writing, and/or math for your school, district, region, and/or state.

Q: **What is the focus of the rest of the coaching conversations over the next six months?**

A: Your 100-day leadership project plan provides the main focus for each coaching conversation. Each conversation begins with your coach listening to you as you describe how your commitments have been going. Each conversation ends with clarity about what you will do in your leadership role between now and the next coaching session. Your coach will ask you to e-mail your updated 100-day leadership project to him or her at the end of each session.

Q: **Will my coach use a process to guide each phone call?**

A: Yes. Although by their nature, coaching conversations are not linear, five phases will lead you to action:

> **Phase I: Begin with greetings and opening questions:** "How did things turn out for you regarding the actions you committed to at the end of our previous call?" "Shall we focus our coaching session on the next actions in your 100-day project plan?" Or, "Do we need to revise in order to focus on new issues that have come up related to this project?"
>
> **Phase II: Tell the story to clarify the current issue:** Your coach will do this by using three tools: (1) listening; (2) asking clarifying and detail questions; and (3) summarizing.
>
> **Phase III: Interaction:** Your coach will ask mediating questions which will help you deepen your thoughts. Your coach

will also voice theories about what might be happening, which may challenge your assumptions and lead you to greater insights.

Phase IV: Status-check and brainstorm actions: Your coach will ask you what you are thinking now that you've had a chance to deepen your understanding through the coaching process. Your conversation will turn to what you want to do now. You may generate many options with your coach at this point.

Phase V: Commitment to action: What will you do to move your project forward between now and the next coaching call? Actions will be specific to your project and will fall into many categories including, but not limited to: learning something new or deepening existing knowledge and skills, analyzing data and evidence, responding to attitudes and cultural issues, and making decisions.

Q: How many months will I have my coach? How many conversations will I have?

A: Generally, you will have your coach for six months. Each month, you will have two coaching conversations which last between 50 and 60 minutes.

Q: What is the schedule for the coaching sessions?

A: Your coach will communicate the coaching schedule with you. Most coaches will schedule a full complement of 12 coaching sessions with you. **Your coach will give you his or her contact information so you can contact the coach on the scheduled days and at the scheduled times.**

Q: What happens if I miss a session?

A: Missed coaching sessions are not rescheduled. In the event you miss a session, your coaching resumes with the next scheduled session.

Q: How do you assign coaches? Will their background match my position?

A: All of our coaches are associates with The Leadership and Learning Center. Some are also practitioners in schools and districts. They have rich backgrounds and experience in education as teachers and administrators from K–12 to the university level. Variables that influence coach assignments include background, experience, and availability.

Q: Will I ever meet with my coach in person?

A: Your coaching will usually occur via the telephone, although some coaches may ask you if you are interested in using SKYPE. Not only does this keep our clients' costs down, but the coaching session itself is focused, efficient, and effective. Unless other arrangements are made, you call your coach at the appointed time and at the phone number your coach provides to you.

Q: How can I get the most out of my coaching experience?

A: (1) Send your 100-day leadership plan to your coach. Update it monthly and have it in front of you during each call. (2) Put your coaching dates on your calendar and make them a priority in your schedule. (3) Attend your coaching sessions. (4) Tell your leadership team/faculty about your coaching project and ask them to give you feedback about how you are doing. (5) Answer this question: "How will I use what happens in coaching to benefit my organization?"

Q: Do I call my coach each time we have a scheduled conversation or does my coach call me?

A: In most cases, for domestic coaching clients you will call your coach at the agreed-upon time. If both you and your coach have stable and reliable Internet connections, your coach may talk to you about using SKYPE.

Sample Coaching Agreement

This agreement between Coach *[insert name]* and Coachee *[insert name]* will begin in *[start month and year]* and end in *[end month and year]*.

Description:

- Coaching, which is not advice, consulting, therapy, or counseling, is designed to support the client in achieving a significant leadership project to create an outcome that invites learning for the leader and benefits the organization. The coach will not provide solutions, or tell the client what to do.
- Throughout the coaching relationship, the client and coach will focus conversations on an important leadership project the client identifies.

Agreements:

Agreements of the Coach	Agreements of the Coachee
• Preserve confidentiality. • Listen, ask clarifying and mediating questions, make observations, and respond for the good of the client. • Schedule the agreed-upon coaching sessions, which usually last for one hour each. • Ask the coachee for feedback about how coaching is working for them. • Use the 100-day project to focus the coaching relationship.	• Identify an important leadership project and come prepared to talk about it. • Follow through on commitments and take action between each coaching conversation. • Participate in the scheduled coaching sessions. Missed sessions are not rescheduled. • Create a 100-day project in order to focus the coaching on accomplishing something important to the organization.

Evaluation and Follow-up:

- At the end of each conversation, the coach asks the coachee to say whether or not the experience was valuable and allowed him or her to identify action to move the project forward.

- The coach makes final notes in the coaching journal for each session and summarizes the actions committed to by the coachee (and the coach, if any). This summary is usually sent to the coachee in a follow-up e-mail so that the coachee has the information in writing and can easily recall and reflect on his or her intentions. Our signatures on this agreement indicate full understanding of and agreement with the information outlined above.

Client Signature:

Date:

Coach Signature:

Date:

Sample Template for Coaching Journal

Replicate this template in a word processing program and start a new one for each person you coach under a coaching agreement (not just a single conversation). Allow the fields to expand as you type.

What observations do you have? What strikes you about this conversation? This might be insights or new questions for you about coaching.	What happened during the conversation? Write just enough so you can re-create the call in your mind the next time you look at your notes. OR, copy and paste the e-mail notes you send to coachees into the space provided (let fields expand as needed).
Conversation 1. Date:	**Conversation 1. Date:**
	Did this call accomplish what you hoped it would?
Conversation 2. Date:	**Conversation 2. Date:**
	Did this call accomplish what you hoped it would?

References

Adams, M. G. (2009). *Change your questions, change your life: 10 powerful tools for life and work.* San Francisco: Berrett-Koehler Publishers, Inc.

Allison, E. (2008, Winter). Coaching teachers for school transformation. *Principal Matters,* Australia.

Allison, E. (2009). Introduction to coaching. *The Reeves report.* www.leadandlearn.com/coaching.

Allison, E. (2010a). *The foundations of great coaching for sustainable change and a greater good.* Salem, MA: Orange Dog Press.

Allison, E. (2010b). Leadership performance coaching: Coach Development Program. Englewood, CO: Lead + Learn Press.

Apatow, R. (1998). *The spiritual art of dialogue: Mastering communication for personal growth, relationships, and the workplace.* Rochester, VT: Inner Traditions International.

Argyris, C. (1993). *Knowledge for action.* San Francisco: Jossey-Bass.

Axtell, P. (2002a). *Coaching skills: A fundamental approach for supporting others.* Moline, IL: Contextual Program Designs.

Axtell, P. (2002b). *Listen . . . Just Listen.* Moline, IL: Contextual Program Designs.

Axtell, P. (2009). *How to be a great coach.* Moline, IL: Contextual Program Designs.

Bloom, G., Castagna, C., Moir, E., & Warren, B. (2005). *Blended coaching: Skills and strategies to support principal development.* Thousand Oaks, CA: Corwin Press.

Bossidy, L., & Charan, R. (2002). *Execution: The discipline of getting things done.* New York: Crown Business.

Braun, L. (2009). *In case of emergency, ask question.* USA: Thought Partners International.

Chen, C. (2003). *Coaching training.* Alexandria, VA: ASTD Press.

Costa, A., & Garmston, R. (1994). *Cognitive coaching: A foundation for renaissance schools.* Norwood, MA: Christopher-Gordon Publishing.

Dufour, R., & Eaker, R. (1998). *Professional learning communities at work: Best practices for enhancing student achievement.* Bloomington, IN: Solution Tree.

Fullan, M. (2001). *Leading in a culture of change.* San Francisco: Jossey-Bass.

Fullan, M. (2009). *Motion leadership: The skinny on becoming change savvy.* Thousand Oaks, CA: Corwin Press.

Goldsmith, M., & Lyons, L. (Eds.). (2006). *Coaching for leadership.* San Francisco: John Wiley and Sons.

Goldsmith, M., & Reiter, M. (2007). *What got you here won't get you there: How successful people become even more successful.* New York: Hyperion.

Haneberg, L. (2006). *Coaching basics.* Alexandria, VA: ASTD.

Hargrove, R. A. (2007). *The masterful coaching fieldbook: Grow your business, multiply your profits, win the talent war!* San Francisco: John Wiley and Sons.

International Coach Federation. (2008). ICF Professional Coaching Core Competencies. www.coachfederation.org/includes/media/docs/CoreCompEnglish.pdf.

Isaacs, W. (1999*). Dialogue and the art of thinking together: A pioneering approach to communicating in business and life.* New York: Doubleday.

Joyce, B., & Showers, B. (1995). *Student achievement through staff development.* White Plains, NY: Longman.

Kilburg, R. R. (2000). *Executive coaching: Developing managerial wisdom in a world of chaos.* Washington, DC: American Psychological Association.

Kilburg, R. R., & Diedrich, R. C. (Eds.). (2007). *The Wisdom of coaching: Essential papers in consulting psychology for a world of change.* Washington, DC: American Psychological Association.

Kouzes, J. M., & Pozner, B. Z. (2003). *The leadership challenge.* San Francisco: Jossey-Bass.

Landsberg, M. (2003). *The tao of coaching.* London: Profile Books.

Marquardt, M. (2005). *Leading with questions.* San Francisco: Jossey-Bass.

Mezirow, J. (2000). Learning to think as an adult: Core concepts of transformation theory. In Mezirow & Associates (Eds.), *Learning as transformation* (pp. 3–34). San Francisco: Jossey-Bass.

Nichols, M. (1995). *The lost art of listening: How learning to listen can improve relationships.* New York: The Guilford Press.

O'Neill, M. B. (2000). *Executive coaching with backbone and heart: A systems approach to engaging leaders with their challenges.* San Francisco: Jossey-Bass.

Pricewaterhouse Coopers (PwC). (2009). ICF global coaching client study. Available at www.coachfederation.org/research.

Reeves, D. (2007, October). Leading to change: Coaching myths and realities. *Educational Leadership, 65*(2).

Reeves, D. B., & Allison, E. (2009). *Renewal coaching: Sustainable change for individuals and organizations.* San Francisco: Jossey-Bass.

Reeves, D. B., & Allison, E. (2010). *Renewal coaching workbook.* San Francisco: Jossey-Bass.

Reiss, K. (2007). *Leadership coaching for educators: Bringing out the best in school administrators.* Thousand Oaks, CA: Corwin Press.

Sanders, L. (2009). *Every patient tells a story: Medical mysteries and the art of diagnosis.* New York: Random House.

Senge, P. M., Ross, R., Smith, B., Roberts, C., & Kleiner, A. (1994). *The fifth discipline fieldbook: Strategies and tools for building a learning organization.* New York: Doubleday.

Stoltzfus, T. (2008). *Coaching questions: A coach's guide to powerful asking skills.* Virginia Beach, VA: Tony Stoltzfus.

Tracy, B. (2006). Making the transition from executive to executive coach. In M. Goldsmith & L. Lyons (Eds.), *Coaching for leadership* (pp. 100–108). San Francisco: John Wiley and Sons.

Ulrich, D. (2006). Coaching the coaches. In M. Goldsmith & L. Lyons (Eds.), *Coaching for leadership* (pp. 145–152). San Francisco: John Wiley and Sons.

Vanderburg, M., & Stephens, D. (2010). The impact of literacy coaches. *The Elementary School Journal, III*(1), 141–163.

Watkins, M. D. (2003). *The first 90 days: Critical success strategies for new leaders at all levels.* Boston: Harvard Business School Publishing.

Whitworth, L., Kimsey-House, H., & Sandahl, P. (1998). *Co-Active coaching.* Palo Alto, CA: Davies-Black Publishing.

Index